CULTURE SHOCK

Copyright © 2017 by Elana Rubin

All Rights Reserved. No portion of this book may be reproduced in any form without permission from the author, except as permitted by U.S. copyright law.

The events described within this book are the author's personal thoughts and recollections of experiences over time. Although the author has made every effort to ensure that the information in this book was correct at press time, the author hereby disclaims any harm caused by errors or omissions.

Cover Design by Veronica Chen

Printed by CreateSpace in the United States of America

First Edition
ISBN-13: 978-1542642699
ISBN-10: 1542642698

For comments and questions, the author can be contacted at cultureshockamemoir@gmail.com.

CULTURE SHOCK

ELANA RUBIN

To North Oaks —

"If you will it,
it is no dream"

For Mom, Dad, Benny, and Tamara.

Without you, I'd have nothing to write about. That being said, sorry! You're in this book a lot!

Acknowledgements

I can literally say that I would not be here today without the people who have helped me. That is, had my great grandfather not survived many perilous obstacles, there would be no book honoring his memory nor anyone to write it for that matter. I thank him for sacrificing his safety to provide me with a better life.

Returning to the present world, thank you Zayde and Manny for giving me your time, patience, and email addresses to ask the many questions and confusions I have about our family history. Thank you especially to Zayde for acting as a volunteer editor. I hope I did your story justice. I also want to thank my cousin Ari and Bube for sharing your stories with me.

Thanks to my parents, not only for giving me the opportunity to live and write this book, but by insisting on reading my stories, allowing me to interview you, understanding when I can't share my work, and reminding me, that yes, I am only eighteen years old. Thank you Tamara and Benny for reminding me that I am a forty-year-old trapped in an eighteen-year-old body.

A huge thanks to my mentor Alice Gartner. You approached this project with the enthusiasm I needed to keep me moving and motivated. I make no exaggeration when I say that without you, I would have been lost in a sea of history, memories, and facts. Thank you for your patience and encouragement.

Thank you to Veronica Chen for the most beautiful cover I have ever seen!

Thank you to the Literary Arts class of 2017. You are my editors, my inspiration, and my family. And Ms. Supplee, where do I begin? You have taught me, guided me, and encouraged me to love imperfection. Your insight has not only pushed me as a writer, but also helped me to grasp who I am. I give as much gratitude as I can muster for the last four years.

And lastly, but most importantly, thank you reader, for giving this book a chance.

The best way to find out if you can trust somebody is to trust them.

—*Ernest Hemingway*

I don't speak because I have the power to speak; I speak because I don't have the power to remain silent.

—*Rabbi A.Y. Kook*

I live in a crazy time.

—*Anne Frank*

Author's Note

This book is called *Culture Shock* because I've realized that most of my personal history consists of coping with uncomfortable change and the unknown. The essay entitled "Culture Shock," demonstrates the first of these changes that drastically altered the person I was set to become: when I was in sixth grade, I moved to Israel for a year. This event, along with the events that followed, became a topic on which I wrote obsessively. Finally, after sorting through journals and blog posts, recalling moments that had been untouched for five years, I wrote this book with a full understanding of what happened to me.

That would have been nice. You would get to read about a journey of self-discovery, how I stomped all my demons into the dust, while developing firm beliefs on Judaism and Israel, ready to enter adulthood as a valuable member of society. If I've learned anything from writing this book, and I've learned more than I thought there was to know, it's that digging usually just leads to more questions.

In eighth grade, I took a trip to Israel with my class. Jet-lagged, and awake for nearly forty-eight hours, we got off the plane and went straight to an archeological dig. The sun hurt our eyes until we climbed into a cool cave and sifted through dirt for pieces of ancient pottery. The archeological site had been open to tourists for years, and still, people found artifacts that ended up in museums.

When I started this book, I expected that by the end, I would understand my feelings, my positions, and myself. But, as a teenager, I am constantly changing; my views ebb to and fro based on the day or the weather. I consider this book like the descent into that cave, combing my shovel and hands through dirt.

I took my life in front of me and sifted: Jewish day school, friendships, disillusion, acne, and faith. There I found my family, and dug deeper: shtetl life, my great grandfather's multiple skirmishes with death, driving a jitney in Atlantic City. Unsure of what I was looking for, but knowing I had not yet found it, I gathered all of Israeli history and laid it out for sieving. This book contains what I've come up with—the riches in this thousand year soil.

Table of Contents

Culture Shock 1

To Life (L'Chaim) 26

A Poor Jew from Russia 37

Some Jewish History: Abraham to Exodus 47

Believing the Bible 50

Family Heirlooms 58

SJH: King Saul to Persian Empire 69

Everything Under the Sun 71

The Fight 81

Long Lost 94

SJH: Alexander the Great to Non-Muslim Restrictions ... 104

Jew-ish 107

Sunrise, Sunset 128

SJH: Crusades to Ottoman Empire 145

On Stories 147

SJH: First Aliyah to White Papers 155

A Body of Land 158

SJH: Holocaust to Munich Olympics 172

Aliyah 176

The Invention of the Wheel 193

Safety and Terrorism 214

Where I'm From 236

Notes 255

Culture Shock

When I was in fifth grade and my father's academic sabbatical neared, my parents announced a decision about the future of their children. I dismissed their plans, even as my father flew to Israel to visit public schools, my parents sent our Israeli friends apartment hunting, and we packed everything but our winter clothes. It wasn't until the tickets were purchased and I told my teachers that I wouldn't need my summer work for sixth grade that I believed them.

For the next few months, my parents were too busy to help us with homework. They leased an apartment, rented our house to a family with young children, and placed our old sick dog, Mendl, in the care of the woman who cleaned our house. In my final days as a fifth grader, my writing workshop teacher brought me out to the hallway and suggested I start a blog. I promised I would. The night before, my family sat down to a spaghetti dinner as my father played the national anthem on the computer, a final salute to our lives in the States. We woke up early, stuffed our fifteen suitcases into the private car, and drove to the BWI airport to catch our connection in Newark. My parents reminded us it was only for a year.

Israel was not a foreign country. My father lived there for five years as a child and was supposed to have stayed for the rest of his life. He told us stories of his apartment in Haifa and the neighbors his family still corresponds with today. In the lobby, he and the other children in the building played *gogoim*, tossing apricot pits down the hallway in competition for the farthest distance. This was not my first trip to Israel either. I visited the country for the first time at seven years old, hitting all the tourist attractions. We visited the Western Wall, watched our step around Mini Israel, shopped in the glow of Ben Yehuda Street at night, and ate falafel every day. We stopped by my father's old apartment, our pockets filled with apricot pits. Thirty years before, when Israel was a young country, the apartment complex had been a new building. Now the bricks were weathered down with cracks; the lights were dim in the hallway where he used to play.

The country is still young but has matured, like a young entrepreneur who washes his hands of dirt and abandons the plow for a desk overlooking the city. Israel is known for the first solar window, cherry tomatoes, the PillCam, and recently, a straw that changes color when a drink has been drugged. The country has grown in confidence, in a fast-paced modern setting that diminishes traditional communal living and transforms *Kibbutzim* from founding settlements of a developing nation to private businesses that rent out cottages to visitors. My

Culture Shock

parents secured a penthouse apartment in Ramat Aviv Gimel, where "frechot"[1] and "arsim"[2] roam the malls in designer clothing, a view that likely stems from the television show "Ramat Aviv Gimel," known as Israel's first telenovela.

    I wrote my first blog post on the airplane. Tuesday, August 17, 2010: "Today I'm going to Israel. This is my first entry of my year trip in Israel. I'm just going to say, that if every day is this adventurous, I'm going to have a lot to write about." I described how our flight to Newark had been delayed forty minutes and landed half an hour after the estimated time of arrival. With fifteen suitcases, we missed the bus to our terminal by taking the elevator. We arrived at our gate late, and the airline agent told us we had to go around the cafeteria to the other entrance. I complained that I was out of breath and my stomach hurt. I signed off optimistically, promising "to try to be excited" and to become fluent in Hebrew, trusting my father's word that I would be fluent within a month.

    Now sleep deprived for two days, we rolled nearly our entire possessions through the automatic doors and stepped into the Holy Land. The heat was heavy and clung to our backs like eucalyptus sap. Men in jeans and collared shirts hollered for taxis in the smoky terminal. Our family and a few other Israelis climbed into a van, and our year in Israel began as Tel

---

[1] Slang for a tan, bedazzled, heavily made-up Israeli woman; think *Jersey Shore* of the Middle East
[2] The male version

Aviv came into view from the highway. We stopped in front of a sand colored apartment building surrounded by palm trees and bushes with fuchsia lotuses: our new home, Avshalom Haviv 6. My mother remarked that it was nearly one hundred degrees.

My room was smaller, just big enough to fit a full bed, a mirror, and an armoire. A mechanical switch on the wall controlled the window blind. At night, the moon glowed through the light canvas, and I saw my friends' faces, the white archway in my backyard, Mendl sprawled on a sunny spot on the carpet. Ramat Aviv Gimel was a ten-minute drive from Tel Aviv, a city alive the whole night with music, dancing, and foot volleyball. I fell asleep to the city rushing beneath me. The cars never stopped.

I wrote my second entry the next day. I worried about communicating at school. I said our apartment was too nice, "Well, too nice for my siblings, anyway. They were doing somersaults on their beds and obstacle courses in a room with really nice furniture. The view is AMAZING." But it didn't feel like home. We were visiting our school the next day, and I hoped it would be full of "nice" kids.

The second night, I didn't sleep. Eventually, I climbed upstairs to the living room, which was decorated with modern sculptures, red and blue velvet couches, and a small collection of books on architecture. I curled up on the blue couch with a volume on Frank Lloyd Wright. In the morning, I went back to my room to get ready to meet my class.

Culture Shock

Our street was a block from the Shufersal market, a ten-minute walk from the Schuster shopping center, and fifteen minutes from the public school. In Baltimore, the car ride to school had been eighteen minutes.

Our parents showed us the walk to school, which was surrounded by a gate that a security guard was instructed to keep locked at all times. In the basement, among the classrooms, was a room full of mice and chinchillas. Outside, a large cage held a family of bunny rabbits. Benny and Tamara, who were entering third grade, quickly found their teachers and began chattering with other students. I met my teacher, Gila, a tough lady with white hair and a kind smile. The students called their teachers by their first name, which was too strange for me, so I avoided saying any names at all, beginning sentences with "Excuse me," and "Um." Gila introduced me to Lior, a tall girl with long dark hair, who shook my hand warmly. She was shy. She couldn't stand in front of people without shaking, hiding her face in her hands. I sat next to her as the rest of my classmates stumbled into the room. They were loud and curious, dressed in the latest European fashions. The girls wore their hair in buns and high waisted shorts with tights and sandals.

While my father was a dual Israeli citizen, my siblings, my mother, and I only had tourist visas. This allowed a stay of three months, so the plan was to obtain visas for a longer stay upon our arrival. We took the number twenty-seven bus to the Ministry of

Interior. We waited three hours for our number to be called. My mother came to the booth and explained our situation in English. The official rudely insisted that acquiring visas for a longer stay would not be possible. I was scared, but probably more excited, that we might have to leave Israel. My father explained in the Israeli style (raised voice, exaggerated hand gestures) that our entire family was here, and he was a visiting professor at the University. After an exchange of unpleasantries, the man announced that my mother must prove that she was Jewish. This required a certified letter from our rabbi, an original copy of her marriage license, and any other documented confirmation of Jewish blood. My siblings and I couldn't get visas because our father was an Israeli citizen, which according to Israeli law, also made us citizens. Therefore, we could not leave the country without Israeli passports. My parents tried to register us as Israeli citizens, but without proof that our mother was Jewish, we could not be considered Jewish either.[3]

My father was told to go to the Jewish Agency of Israel in Jerusalem to obtain a certification stamp for the rabbi's letter. There was a Tel Aviv address, but the Jerusalem agency did not know it. Once again at the Ministry of Interior, another official explained that my mother could not get a visa for spouses and

---

[3] According to Jewish law, Judaism is passed down through the mother

children because my father was Israeli. My parents took another number to wait for an extended tourist visa. They considered taking a vacation outside of Israel every two and a half months, renewing my mother's visa every three months. Of course, the children wouldn't be allowed to leave the country, so they had no choice but to find the Ministry of "Controlling Who is Jewish."[4]

My parents tried to take a taxi, but the taxi driver told them that the building was five minutes away, and they should walk. My father reminded the driver that he was paying him. The building turned out to be the Tel Aviv address for the Jewish Agency of Israel. However, the woman in charge was in Jerusalem to prepare for Rosh Hashanah and would not return until Tuesday.

Two days later, the Jewish Agency called my mother to say that the building was closing in twenty minutes and she had to pick up the rabbi's letter. My mother arrived to find that none of the documents had been certified. The officials worked quickly, and she received the certified proof of her Judaism with enough time to go back to the Ministry of Interior before it closed for the day. When my father arrived, she was filling out a visitor visa form. The "pending verification" status of the children's Judaism was lifted. My father shook hands with the man behind the desk. So far, the year did not hold much promise.

---

[4] As my father put it

On Tuesday, September 7, 2010, I wrote: "We've been in Israel for three weeks. So, I've already started school. On the first day, I'm not even sure how I managed to survive." I wrote about how I usually woke up early on the first day of school, excited to meet friends, teachers, and learn the coursework. Other years, I woke up early filled with dread about homework, confusing lessons, and mean kids. "This year, I somehow managed to sleep in. Probably, from not sleeping the whole night, or because I was hoping the day would never start."

My parents walked me to school. Immediately, a group of girls saw me and asked to sit with me. "Anywhere you go, in Israel or America, everybody wants to meet the new kid," I wrote. The day turned out to be confusing. The girl I sat next to knew English well enough to translate for me, but I was dizzy listening to shouts, the different teachers walking in and out the door, the boards filled with Hebrew. "I can't tell you how many times I looked at my watch, told myself not to look at my watch because I did a second ago, and asked what was going on."

After that first day, I was handed the responsibility of making sure my siblings made it to school in one piece. Considering that I was dragged into a different culture, any added obligations felt like a personal attack. I would be herding sheep, which hadn't been a popular job in Israel for hundreds of years. I sat Benny and Tamara down and informed them that if they weren't ready on my time, I would leave without them. Every morning they woke up late, ate breakfast sluggishly, and decided to pack their bags and lunches after I had been standing by the door for five minutes, yelling at them. I warned them we would be late the entire walk.

My father, who as a three year old had not been concerned with accents or embarrassment, was fluent in Hebrew. I had been in the highest Hebrew class in my Jewish day school, but enrolling in Israeli public school was a different beast. My siblings and I needed tutoring every afternoon. Our first tutor was a heavily perfumed ex-school teacher with bleached hair and floral shirts. She led us to the back of her house to a small room, where she talked us through children's book renditions of Bible stories we already knew and taught us Hebrew we had reviewed years before. After a few weeks, we staged a strike, and my parents found a new tutor. Roni was young and patient. She came to our house every afternoon after school and became a close friend.

I watched silently for most of the year. When the students spoke out of turn and talked back, the teachers yelled at them. Sixth grade was still elementary school; we sat in the same chairs while teachers for different subjects rotated among us. They were tough Israelis who knew how to discipline rowdy Israeli children. Not knowing I was new and American, they barked fast commands at me that I didn't understand. I came away from class breathing heavily, wiping tears from my eyes. I was shy, with skin thin as tissue paper. I often cried in my room.

The school was an odd collection of personalities who came together to keep the children occupied and intact. My gym teacher was an opera singer. He had us run around the school and called out our times as we collapsed in front of him, panting. He once sent me outside to run in the rain before I had time to stretch. My running times were similar to those of the Israelis, but when the coach called out the names of those traveling to other schools to run meets, I was never called. I told everyone he was anti-American, even though he had lived in New Jersey, and I had never asked to run. My sister's teacher was an ex-model from the Czech Republic. She smoked in the courtyard, wore Aladdin-style gypsy pants, taught my science class, and was the favorite teacher of the third grade. My brother's teacher had a nose job and a lip injection and thought that Benny had a learning disability because he said the homework was too hard for him. My brother got away with not doing homework for a month and a half. The principal was new that year, and my grade hated him. He once took me aside and asked "Isn't Baltimore violent?" I said I lived in the suburbs, half an hour from the city.

"But are you sure it's safe?" he asked. I told him it was. Curiously enough, when we returned to America, our neighbors had been arrested for the drug lab in their basement. A girl my age who lived on the next street reported an attempted kidnapping and a robbery while she was still home. I worried excessively that I was missing important events back home. I Skyped with my friends from home, and they told me about their exciting plans and busy school life. I began to imagine my place back at school and visualized the same metaphor every night. I was like a tree that had been cut down, a building constructed on top of it. If the tree grew back, it would be unwanted and out of place.

Slowly, we settled into routine. The school day had two breaks. The first half was for eating snacks from home, which was often pita and chocolate spread, or as many of my peers liked to eat, an egg sandwich with pickle. I tried this at home once and had to lie in my bed for an hour to let the nausea subside. The second half was for free time, when the sixth graders found the first grade mentees they had been assigned to. I held my first graders' hands as we circled the building, passing a garden, a sports court, and a playground. It was a relief to speak to younger children who didn't recognize my American accent and limited vocabulary. The girl chattered away, while every few minutes the little boy let out a sigh, saying, "I'm bored." I started bringing them candy, and they looked forward to greeting me outside. Eventually, they hugged me one last time and ran off into the playground with their friends. School ended by one fifteen, and I walked my siblings home to eat lunch and start our tutoring sessions. The only day off was Saturday, Shabbat, when my family rode our bikes along the beach. There, we locked our bikes, bought fresh squeezed lemonade and fresh fruit from the market, and watched the waves.

Benny and Tamara made friends quickly and had play dates after school. Tamara and I took jewelry making classes after school. Benny started taking chess lessons and participated in tournaments against Tamara's best friend. My father conducted research at Tel Aviv University and rode his bike to work every day. Meanwhile, my mother began taking Hebrew lessons at the Ulpan.[5] Once, when my school held a field day, my mother let me skip to come with her. We rode a bus and entered a building that looked suspiciously like a high school, with rows of desks lining classrooms and bulletin boards with construction paper hanging on the wall. As my mother took out her pen and notebook paper, I sat on a bench outside her classroom and read a book.

My parents signed us up for piano lessons, which we had been taking since we were five years old. At first, they hired the music teacher from my school, a Russian man who didn't speak English and smelled so terrible that I couldn't concentrate. The theme of the year: we tried again. Our next piano teacher was young and pregnant. She offered us walnuts and water as we waited for all three of us to finish our lessons.

---

[5] An institute designed to teach adult immigrants Hebrew language skills.

Culture Shock

She taught me the "Fur Elise" and "Ballet Pour Adeline."

From the beginning of the school year and continuing into the summer, the Israeli girls celebrated their Bat Mitzvahs at the age of twelve. They did not have a service. If they were Orthodox, they were not allowed to read Torah, and if they were secular, they threw large parties instead. A few hours before the first party started, a girl from my class called me and asked if I was going. I told her I wasn't.

"You should," she said. She talked to my dad in Hebrew for a few minutes and told me she would come and get me in an hour, informing me to wear jeans and a cute top. Only the Bat Mitzvah girl wore a dress. I slinked by the chips and popcorn tables while my classmates danced and flirted. At one point, the DJ stopped the party, and a group of girls surrounded the Bat Mitzvah girl, who wore a sundress and a tiara, and they began to perform a choreographed dance. The parties blended together: a crowded room of relatives, soft drinks, loud music that popped my ears. The only differences were the room, the girl, and the dress. In the middle of the year, I stopped attending Bat Mitzvah parties.

Then the girls invited me to have lunch with them in the Schuster center on Friday afternoons. My father walked me to the restaurant. I took the English menus and ate silently as they chattered rapidly in Hebrew, only speaking when they asked me questions directly. We went to get ice cream. After finishing my cone, I walked home by myself. That night, my parents said I couldn't have dessert because I'd already had ice cream, and I cried that I could only communicate with my classmates through eating. "Someday you'll appreciate this," my dad said.

I saw his face. He was disappointed I was having a hard year. He wanted to see me happy, but this was also his year. He had been granted a Fulbright scholarship. He was giving a nearly impossible opportunity to his children. The crying, the complaining, the unhappiness: this was not what he imagined.

As much as I complained about my lack of social life, I was a shy girl, ridden with insecurities that kept me clammed up in the back of the classroom, unable to reach out for friendship. I was embarrassed by my American accent, so I didn't speak Hebrew to my classmates. I was in an advanced English class, but I still had to take standard Israeli English. I was bored learning words like "fire" and "baker" and reading paragraphs about rats. I scored one hundred percent on all of my grammar tests, while the teacher tried to catch a mistake to prove I didn't know English as well as I thought I did. When my cousin visited and came with me to school, the teacher told her in clear Hebrew, "Elana doesn't really know Hebrew."

The advanced English class was led by a young American woman with blonde hair. The five students, four boys and myself, met in the library. One of the boys hated me. He interrogated me about my shyness,

Culture Shock

asking me if I even talked, while I stammered and tried not to cry. Later, he was suspended for three days for throwing a chair at the geography teacher. For a few weeks, the teacher came into class with a cut on his nose.

One time, a group of Israeli boys, including the boy from my English group, who usually walked on the other side of the sidewalk, followed me home from school, cursing and shouting in Hebrew. I looked back only once to see their faces. I told my siblings to keep walking, and we nearly ran until we reached the crosswalk. I came home and collapsed on my bed, shaking. The boys were not intimidating to the girls in my class, who flirted with them and made them their boyfriends, as I skirted around them and leaned against the wall because I didn't know what to do with my hands.

My first friend was a girl named Einav who looked about fifteen. She invited me to her house every day after school, where she would make me food and use my face as a canvas to practice makeup. It became apparent that I was her only friend. I started making excuses. I had tutoring every day. I was tired. I was going out to eat with my family.

In October, the cleaning lady wrote to say that Mendl had died. I told Einav I didn't want to come over. She insisted on walking me to my apartment anyway, saying, "Maybe the cleaning lady did something to make him sick."

"He had cancer," I said.

"Still," she said. "You weren't there." I cried in the elevator. The crying became part of my daily routine, like combing my hair and brushing my teeth. I waited throughout the day, closer to the evening, when I knew I could be alone. Then I shut myself in my room and confronted every detail that had made me hold back tears: jokes about my accents, breaks I spent alone or petting animals with my brother, ashamed to be the oldest one in the room.

After Einav forced me into a chair, wet my hair and put green eye shadow on me, I never went back. Eventually she stopped asking. My mother took me to a photo store, where I bought a bulky brown leather scrapbook. I decorated five scrapbook pages in memory of my dog before I abandoned the project.

My father tried to get me more involved. His next move was the Tzofim, the Israeli Scouts. I protested as he took a picture of me in my uniform, a beige button up with a blue handkerchief around my neck. We wore iron-on badges. We gave salutes. We played games, we painted, we had campouts. I followed along, uncomfortable with cheering, racing my classmates, and trying to follow the Hebrew commands. One night, I came home crying after an older boy accidently threw a tomato at me during an activity. It was an accident, but he didn't apologize. I hated tomatoes. My parents finally agreed not to make me go back.

In my defense, the isolation wasn't entirely of my own making. My city was secular, and the kids didn't keep kosher. They talked about cheeseburgers and snails they tried in France. When I showed them pictures from my Jewish Day School's website, they were confused that the boys were wearing yarmulkes.

"You are Orthodox?" a girl asked me.

"Conservative," I said. They didn't know what that was. Later another girl asked me if I celebrated Christmas because I was American.

On Yom Kippur, we were one of the only families fasting. The national law stated that people could not drive cars, so the streets were filled with bikes. It was just a day off. The children rode tricycles behind their parents, who did not wear helmets and rode without holding the handle bar. We weaved through the crowd on our bikes to services, and then spent the rest of the day in our beds, weak from dehydration and empty stomachs.

Our small congregation met in the community center in the park, until we moved to the building where my brother took chess lessons. The rabbi was an American who had made Aliyah to Israel. He had a large family and kept Shabbat. He invited us for Shabbat dinner at his house, cluttered with toys. The children led me to their room and showed off their bookshelf. I mentioned that I hadn't read Harry Potter.

"Here," one of the children said. "You can borrow it."

So every few Saturdays when we went to services, they pulled the next book from their little sister's baby carriage, and I read the entire series in a few months. I spent most days isolated in my room, reading the longest books I could download on my Mom's iPhone. I distracted myself with *David Copperfield* for a few weeks.

Reading helped me keep a piece of home with me. I could be anywhere I wanted for a matter of hours. I felt lonely only after finishing a book. Starting a new one meant meeting new faces, learning new mannerisms, growing comfortable with the uncomfortable. I had done that too many times.

I told myself I was going to be organized. I made a daily schedule, designating time to eat, do homework, read, and practice piano. I surrounded myself with rules and structure. I decided I didn't need friends.

Instead, I wrote about big ideas in my laptop, stayed up until four in the morning surfing the web, and watched people. Israelis walked everywhere. They were healthy, eating salad for breakfast, always on the move. They were thin and beautiful, and I knew I didn't fit in. I had acne and filled up on pita and Russian cookies from the Shufersal. Even though we lived in Israel, we still were tourists in a different country. For Hanukah break, we went to the Negev and stayed at a Bedouin camp. My family, who had tried camping once, until it rained and they canceled the trip, preferred to stay in a cabin rather than experience an authentic Bedouin tent. We rode camels, lit the Hanukiah, and ate a homemade meal in the large main tent. It never struck me that we appeared

Culture Shock

like normal American tourists on these trips. I went to Israeli school. I spoke Hebrew. I lived in an apartment overlooking the Tayelet[6]. I considered myself an Israeli.

My fourth and final post before I abandoned my blog was about visiting Max Brenner, a chocolate restaurant. I described everyone's dish in decadent detail. My brother ordered, "A tuna sandwich with a salad and chocolate pizza with gummy bears, marshmallows, and chocolate chips. The chocolate pizza was good, I had a small bite of it because that's all he would give me." I ended the post with a modest boast that I only ordered chocolate milk, and that was the last I wrote about the year.

As the New Year came and winter ushered in, my grandparents rented an apartment from a professional pianist, a ten-minute drive from us. It never got cold. The only place it snowed was Jerusalem. While my siblings and I comfortably walked to school in sweatshirts, Israelis wore mittens and heavy coats. Low temperatures were in the fifty or sixty degrees Fahrenheit range. The atmosphere didn't change: the leaves didn't fall off trees, the flowers stayed in bloom, but the new year brought change I didn't expect.

Lior, the shy girl Gila introduced me to, and I had been allies from the start, but after a few months, we became inseparable. Lior and Shani, my two best friends. Shani was tiny, but she was sassy. She had a

---

[6] The Tel Aviv Promenade that runs along the beach from Tel Aviv to the city of Jaffa

twin sibling named Shir, who was the sweeter of the two. Lior was an athletic runner and a talented artist. Shani was jealous of her. I went to their houses most days after school, and we played "The Sims" for hours and ate Israeli chocolate. I told them about my home back in Baltimore and showed them pictures of my room. I grew to know their parents and their pets. I began going to Bat Mitzvah parties again. My father drove us as we giggled and chatted in the back seat.

My birthday fell on Purim. I made myself a blue and gold necklace and dressed up as Cleopatra. My sister was SpongeBob, and my brother was a ninja. There was a large parade in Tel Aviv, and we got lost in the crowd of costumes and music and food. That night, we returned to Max Brenner per my request, and I ordered a chocolate pizza. My grandparents bought me an art book on Impressionism. For Passover break, we went to the Golan Heights. It was chilly, and we had to wear sweatshirts. We took a ride on a cable car overlooking sloping green landscapes and dotted hills.

In May on Lag BaOmer[7], giant bonfires sparked and the smell of burning wood clogged the air. Lior, Shani, and I joined our classmates in the empty lot next to my apartment building, where they were throwing old newspapers and cardboard boxes into the fire. The bonfire was taller than any fire I'd seen, yet

---

[7] A holiday for rabbinical students, with outdoor sports. Today, it's an excuse to light giant bonfires.

my classmates were fearless, standing in front of the smoke, laughing, sharing food. I smiled as I watched them and followed Lior and Shani away from the crowd, away from the noise and children cheering and playing with fire. We went to Shani's house, where her mother made us pasta. We smelled like smoke. We shared stories and jokes, and I went home late that night when I was usually scared of walking alone in the dark. Bonfires fizzled out as they were drenched with water. I walked home slowly and watched the smoke. It was a comforting smell. I smiled into the darkness.

At the end of the month, we biked to the beach to meet up with the eighth grade class from my middle school, which was taking its annual trip to Israel. I sat on a bench, facing the waves, and spoke to the science teacher I'd had the year before. I had trouble envisioning these two worlds colliding. We talked about my middle school, and I reflected on my year. I said it had been difficult, but I was glad for the experience. I said it for her sake so I didn't appear spoiled. I watched the eighth graders laugh and play in the sand. The beach was beautiful. I'd miss it, I admitted.

At the end of the year, it was time for the graduation ceremony. In the weeks leading up to it, my class split into acting, singing, and dancing acts. I had signed up for acting, but realizing that I wouldn't be able to speak because of my embarrassing American accent, I switched to dance. During rehearsals, I tried to follow along without being seen. Most of the girls were part of a singing group and took dance lessons. I didn't know how to do either. When the night came, we wore white shirts and jeans, carrying around Israeli flags in choreographed formation. Then, I changed into a white top and orange shirt, and we danced to traditional Israeli music. Suddenly, I didn't feel shy or out of place. Under the light, I could not be distinguished from any other Israeli graduating from the sixth grade. Gila handed me my diploma and hugged me. Immediately after, we left for Roni's wedding, and as I sat on the side watching the dance floor, exhausted, I wondered where the time had gone. Home seemed like a different life. I was excited to leave. I was done with the country that had made me miserable that entire year.

Our plane ride was July fifth. We went to the pizza place in the Schuster Center for the last time, watching the sunset. My sister's friend joined us and sobbed as she hugged my sister goodbye. My friends gave me a treasure box, a photo album, and seashell earrings. I thought of buying a chocolate bar and writing "You're so sweet," but I never did. We exchanged email addresses. I hugged them tightly. Then, we drove to the airport. I sat next to my dad on the flight as he dozed off. Unable to sleep, I watched movies until morning. My dad gave me the eggs from his airplane breakfast.

We reached New York at four in the morning, wide awake with excitement. It was the first time I remember feeling happy that year, or the first time I had wanted to be happy all year. We landed in Baltimore late in the morning. When the car pulled up the driveway, and I saw the green of our front lawn, the house's red dusted bricks, the ten trees I'd named, the arch with the stone pathway, the crooked mailbox on the driveway that had been hit by a backward-moving car one too many times, I started crying. I sobbed up the stairs and through the hallway, exhausted and maybe a little delirious. My best friend arrived a few minutes later, and we embraced. I went to her house, awake with adrenaline, and almost fell asleep onto my homemade pizza. I remember the silence on the first night back home. I had grown used to the sounds of the city.

I stood in different rooms throughout the house, where every object remained as we had left it. My bed, with the blue canopy and purple sheets sat in the middle of my room. The pool table remained unused in the room beside the staircase. The worn green couch wrapped around the carpet with acorn designs in the living room. The familiarity of these objects mingled with a foreign feeling. A different person was standing in these rooms.

My family unpacked, and in another month, I packed again for sleep-away camp, where I spent four weeks. I read my books for school and finished my summer work. I exchanged emails with my friends in Hebrew. Slowly, the emails became less frequent. It hit me that I was never going to see them again.

I went back to school, and it felt as if the year had never happened. On the first day of school, we had morning services outside. It was a sunny day. Flowers fell onto our prayer books from the trees. I took a seat, wanting my return to be acknowledged just as much as I wanted to be ignored. I was disappointed when my classmates chatted with their friends and left me sitting silently. One girl asked me if I wanted the honor of reading an Aliyah. I stuttered and stammered in front of her, unable to say the word "no," until she said, gently, "I'll ask someone else." I congratulated myself that I had been right. I was now the tree in the middle of the building, unwanted and out of place. As I sat in the car while my mother drove me to school, I remembered the late nights walking home alone in Israel.

In the next year, we got a new dog, named Gimel in honor of the year we spent in Ramat Aviv Gimel. Sometimes, I sort through a box of old artifacts in my room. I take out the old cell phone with the wrong adapter on the charger, where I took videos of our trips. I feel the weight of the bottles of sand I collected from Eilat and a crater in the Negev. Memories of the year are distant now and will continue to fade. I look at pictures from our trips, a smile on my face. I didn't look particularly unhappy. Then again, I had underestimated the shock of impact crashing into an unfamiliar place, and then the pull of the roots that stretched to blooming flowers, unnoticed, from a quiet garden on the roof of Avshalom Haviv 6.

To Life (L'Chaim)

In the entrance to Ramat Aviv Gimel School are three portraits: a girl with long red hair; an older boy with brown hair; and an adolescent with black hair. These are the alumni who were killed in combat. The adolescent was named Chaim. One night in March, my scouts group held a ceremony for the anniversary of his death. We wore white. Wordlessly, we drifted to the center, where his name was outlined in chalk, and lay down roses. A video montage began to play: pictures of a smiling young man, accompanied by a song that seemed sadder than any I had ever heard. Behind us, his mother sobbed in the bleachers, trying to stifle her sniffles with a wet tissue. I came home shaking.

Later, I looked up the song that played during the ceremony, "Keev Shel Lochamim," which translates to "The pain of the protector." A soldier tries to explain his experiences in war, "And you, you don't know how much I tried to hide from you."

Every day on our way to school, my siblings and I passed an army training camp.

Culture Shock

I once exchanged glances with a soldier who was crossing the street. Her hair was tied in a ponytail, sunglasses on her nose, a cell phone against her ear, and a rifle strapped across her back. She stepped onto the dirt, and we continued down the sidewalk, as if children passing soldiers was the most natural thing in the world. In Israel, it is. Apart from Haredi Jews who study at yeshiva[1], every Israeli teenager goes straight to Tzahal[2] after graduating high school; the army is just another part of life.

Among the commotion of cars, bright spices, and loud music from outdoor cafés, loss permeates the Mediterranean heat. An underlying sentiment, forms in every community: coming to terms with the unthinkable but inevitable. Every child will one day be a soldier. We learned discipline in the Tzofim.[3] We wore uniforms, stood in single file lines, and gave salutes. We learned to normalize threats. In Baltimore, there were fire drills. In Israel, we had bomb drills. A siren went off in the middle of class, and in single file, we descended the stairs to the cramped bomb shelter, which had been converted to a storage space. My classmates laughed and joked around, and the teachers reminded us to remain quiet during drills.

---

[1] An Orthodox Jewish seminary, focusing on the study of traditional religious texts
[2] A Hebrew acronym for the Israeli Defense Forces
[3] An Israeli youth movement comparable to the Boy and Girl Scouts of America

In May, there was a ceremony in the park for Yom HaZikaron, Israel's Memorial Day for fallen soldiers. That night, grieving men and women prayed, sang, and remembered. Families lit rows of candles on a stage. A woman gave a memorial speech, letting her tears fall openly. We bowed our heads and mourned together.

The next night was Yom HaAzmaut, Israel's Independence Day. We wiped away our tears and played Hebrew music. We danced in the streets. We waved Israeli flags. Air Force jets spiraled and flipped above us. Fireworks turned the night sky to daylight. This is Israel. We get up, bandage our bruises, and keep going.

I didn't understand how Israelis could keep going after experiencing loss until a year into my return to the States.

Every summer, my family visited my grandfather in Michigan, where he lived on a lake with his boats. He had a full belly and white stubble from cheek to cheek. He wore sunglasses attached to a string around his neck, steering his motorboat, smiling from a sunburnt face. Sometimes, he let me sit on his lap and steer. Reticent, but kind-hearted, he used to walk me to his neighbor's house to borrow movies, and we watched *The Jungle Book*, *Babe,* and Shirley Temple in *Heidi* on his couch. I played with his train set or cut out paper doll chains from an instruction book. He held barbecues in his backyard, for all the relatives on my mother's side of the family. My cousins and I put on our bathing suits and splashed in the water, running back squealing as my grandfather lifted the top from the hot tub.

We had never been close. He possessed a gruff personality that was matched only by our Yellowstone Park tour guide, who didn't know how to interact with children and invited himself to our lunch table, casually talking of bear attacks while he ate a salmon wrap. My grandfather was standoffish, traveling to Vietnam, China, and Amsterdam on a plumber's salary, bringing back trinkets, dolls, and fans for us the few times a year we saw him. Yet, he took the time to show me the pictures from his most recent trip to China and patiently described that he pricked his finger to keep his blood sugar balanced. Gifts from him were surprisingly thoughtful. He gave me a mini remote control car that charged in a plastic bubble. He gave me a collection of pages I could send in to be made into a book because he knew I loved to write. I must have hugged him a hundred times.

The night my grandfather called to tell us he had been diagnosed with cancer was the night before my last day of seventh grade. It was the talent show, and my friend was supposed to sing while I played the piano. I played the wrong notes, bowed for the applause, and left the room sobbing, digging my nails into my palm.

We visited him that summer, after he had already started chemotherapy. He was so thin I didn't recognize his face. His eyes popped out. They were red and unfocused, darting in every direction like a fearful animal. He cried often. My parents tried to buy him protein smoothies, but he could not be convinced to eat. He lay on the couch for most of the day, covered in a blanket. His bed had been moved to his office because he had trouble climbing the stairs. He went to sleep early. After we heard the door shut behind him, my siblings and I hesitantly gathered on the couch, avoiding the spot where he had slept, and watched the *Harry Potter* marathon on TV.

I spent most of the visit upstairs, reading *Blue Eyed Child of Fortune*, which contained the letters of Colonel Robert Gould Shaw, who led one of the first African-American regiments in the Civil War. I was scared of death, so I was scared of my grandfather. I came downstairs to exchange a few words, and after a few minutes, I hid upstairs again. I went with my father to buy groceries to get out of the house. In the car, I admitted I had trouble being around my grandfather.

"It's going to be difficult," my father said. "There's no way to deal with it."

I could never speak to him by myself. As the family surrounded the couch, he told us he would try to make it to my siblings' B'nei Mitzvah in two years. Then he started crying again, and the kids instinctively backed away. We dispersed, and I went back to my book.

He died in October. My mother, who had flown in a week earlier, was by his side. When the phone rang that night, we knew. The next day in school, I stood during the Mourner's Kaddish[4] and burst into tears in front of my entire grade, mortified. I went to my teacher to tell her I had to catch a flight in a few hours, and I wanted to collect the homework. She hugged me and told me not to worry about it. My father picked us up to take us to the airport, and we flew back to Michigan. We didn't know what to say to each other, exchanging pleasantries about the weather, afraid to bring up the reason for our trip. We rented a car and arrived to his empty house. As we pulled up, my mother's cousin arrived with her kids and brought trays of food into the house. I tried to smile to her children, whom I had only met a few times at my grandfather's barbecues. In a nightmare version of déjà vu, I read my book, we watched television, and we avoided the spot where my grandfather had slept. I woke up early in the mornings and met my father downstairs to cycle the paddle boat silently around the lake. I was afraid to look at my mother.

At his funeral, I could not concentrate on the rabbi's words. I stared at the stained glass window so I wouldn't cry. My grandfather wanted to be cremated, so his coffin was borrowed from the funeral home. At the Shivah, the house was crowded with his friends and neighbors. They spread his ashes around the lake

---

[4] A hymn said as a mourning ritual during all Jewish prayer services. Those who have experienced a loss stand and recite at every service for eleven or twelve months. Everyone else sits and answers.

at my grandfather's request, and we went inside to pray. At the end of the service, a neighbor stood up and shakily held out a box of orange pop-ups.

"I don't know what to do," he said, "but Larry always loved these, and I wanted to share them." He passed around the box, and we sat together, wearing black, sucking on orange pop-ups. I tried not to spill on my skirt. Every few minutes, tears would threaten, and I hid them in the orange liquid spilling down my chin.

The house was easy to sell. My grandfather's artifacts from his travels were divided among the relatives and friends. I picked out a painting he had bought from Vietnam and a Native American quilt. We locked up and left his house, the lake, the boats, for the last time. No more barbeques. No more movies. No more paper doll chains.

Since his death five years ago, I have thought about my grandfather every day. As memories fade, he becomes missing space. The empty house, where my great grandmother, his mother, used to lie on the floor with a blanket before she died. The empty couch where he used to sleep. The cold windows facing the lake, where I drew smiley faces out of my breath on the glass. The missing chair at the Thanksgiving table. I will be walking the hallways at school, running through the neighborhood, aimlessly tapping through the apps on my phone, when a memory, or the absence of memory will hit me, and I have to stop as it takes hold.

Culture Shock

When I returned to school in America, Yom HaZikaron was a normal day. My seventh grade Bible class fidgeted in their seats. They told jokes and giggled.

"Why don't you tell us your experience from Yom HaZikaron in Israel?" the teacher asked me.

"Well," I swallowed. "There were sirens in the middle of class, and we all stood at our desks. And there was a ceremony at night, and they lit candles." I thought about Chaim and his mother trying not to cry on the bleachers.

"I'm sure you are thankful you got to experience that!" the teacher said and flipped to the next slide on her presentation.

"But everyone was laughing and fooling around instead of listening to the siren," I told my friend later.

"Okay," she said. She didn't understand because she didn't know Chaim. I did not know him either, but I still see his mother's tears, the group of girls that surrounds her and takes her hands wordlessly. I see her walking the streets of Tel Aviv, buying groceries in the fresh fruit market on the Tayelet, building up the strength to laugh with friends. I see her stopping, a distant look in her eye, as she hears his laugh, sees him standing before her. She reaches out to touch him, and the memory fades just as quickly. She returns to her present task. She crosses the street, hands a few shekels to the woman behind the cash register, and hopes her smile is wide enough to distract from her eyes.

Every Israeli knows somebody who died in the army. The pain I felt on Yom HaZikaron was a swirling in my chest, an abstraction of incomprehensible emotion. Israelis feel intense, specific loss. Loss has a shape: long brown hair, manicured fingernails, a cousin, a boyfriend, a friend.

Many Israeli children are excited to go to the army. They are tasked with honoring and protecting their country. In Ramat Aviv Gimel, with enlistment still six years away, my class was less concerned with Yom HaZikaron than I had expected. Our teacher read letters from the siblings of soldiers who had died, but my classmates did not seem to hear a word. They scribbled on their desks, or passed notes in the back, or stared at the ceiling with their eyes glazing over. A nationwide siren sounded at 11:00 a.m., and we were instructed to stand at our desks. It blared for two minutes in memoriam. I bowed my head in a moment of silence, while my classmates whispered to each other, giggling behind their hands. By the time the siren ended, the room was filled with loud chatter and shouting. The teacher yelled at us and held up the letters. "Is this how you honor the soldiers who gave their lives?" I came home upset that my classmates had been so disrespectful. My mom told me that Israelis had hard lives. Parents want their children to have happy childhoods before they go the army, where Yom

Culture Shock

HaZikaron becomes all too real. That was something I hadn't thought about before.

Despite my mother's insight, I still thought my class should have been more respectful. But I did not spend my adolescence imagining glory or horror on the battlefield. What would you do if you were an Israeli parent? What would you do if you knew your child would one day join the ranks of grieved or grieving? You would want them to be happy. I recalled a memory from a few weeks before. At Shabbat dinner, over matzah ball soup, the rabbi told us about a girl he was tutoring for her Bat Mitzvah. In a lesson about the Middle East, she interrupted to exclaim, "You mean there are people in the world who aren't Jewish?"

I remembered how the girls at school asked me if I celebrated Christmas the same day they asked if I was an Orthodox Jew. I once left the Tzofim early to go to Shabbat services. Our activity was held outside the entrance to the building where Shabbat goers were beginning to file in. One girl looked at me confused. "You're *praying* in there?" she asked. I nodded and ran inside, feeling uncomfortable.

You wouldn't want them to know anything but happiness.

I will not be going to the army next year with the rest of my class from Ramat Aviv Gimel. As I attend college orientation, they will begin basic training. As I am handed a syllabus, they will be handed assault rifles and uniforms. The façade of their undisturbed childhoods will wash away. They will become soldiers passing unsuspecting children on the sidewalk. Their silence is the pain of the protector: they will protect their country; they will protect the children from seeing themselves in those stiff army boots.

A Poor Jew from Russia

In Belarus, about twelve miles from Minsk, there is a large, but deserted field. In the summer, it is filled with ferns and wild daisies. In the winter, snow falls heavily and covers the ground, exposing only a few young trees. The field is quiet, disregarding the muffled drilling of a woodpecker, the hissing of geese during nesting season, and the memories of a life that doesn't exist anymore.

One hundred years ago. Imagine a circle of small wooden houses surrounding a larger building that is the synagogue. The Rebbe[1] practically lived in this building, though his house was nearby. The synagogue was walking distance from all the houses. Every Saturday, a hundred families put on their nicest clothing and joined together in the room. This town was called Uzlian. My great-great-grandfather, Mordechai Rubenchick was the town's tinsmith, which was a fairly respected job. My great-great-grandmother was illiterate. She woke up at two or

---

[1] Distinguished from other rabbis as the leader of the Hasidic Jewish community

three in the morning to darn socks, keep the house, and care for the chickens and cows.

Uzlian was small, even by the standards of a Jewish shtetl.[2] When he was little, Yaacov Rubenchick, my great-grandfather, started an argument with another kid by saying, "My town is bigger than yours."

The other kid responded, "Your town is so small, it's not even on the map."

As customary in shtetl tradition, my great-great-grandparents had many children, perhaps seven sons and daughters. During the week, the boys studied with the Rebbe by the fireplace as the Russian winds whipped the schoolhouse so that it shuddered. Yaacov was sent to yeshiva at a young age, yet he was the brightest by far. Underneath his open *Gemara*,[3] he read a Russian book, so when the Rebbe turned around, he saw only the cover of the Gemara. Yaacov studied *Tanakh*[4] until he was twelve. By then, he had the whole book memorized, and the Rebbe called on him to help the other students. He knew Torah trope by heart, and although it made him nervous, he often did the *leyenen*.[5]

This bright boy became the man who stands over me every day of my life. I am alive because of a term coined "Rubin luck." Our lives have never crossed, but I see parts of him in myself, accepting

---

[2] A small Jewish village, think *Fiddler on the Roof*
[3] An important piece of Rabbinical commentary
[4] A combination of Torah, Prophets, and Writings
[5] The public reading of the Torah

Culture Shock

Torah readings and solos in my Jewish choir, feeling sick the entire day: sweaty palms and thumping heart and hands that shake so much they can't hold the *yad*[6] in place against the Torah. Yet, we are from completely different worlds. There is no way to recreate the life of Jews during the turn of the twentieth century. All that remains of this lifestyle are songs in commemoration: "Oyfn pripetshik brent a fayerl, Un in shtub iz heys, Un der rebe lernt kleyne kinderlekh, Dem alef-beys." On the hearth, a fire burns, and in the house it is warm, and the rabbi is teaching little children the alphabet.

As much as we venerate the shtetl Jews, we do not long for the olden days. When Yaacov was eighteen, life was tough for Jews. His family had almost nothing: no money, no food, no clothing. Yaacov got ahold of a contraband salami and was coming home in a wagon when the police stopped him. Someone had tipped them off about the salami. They searched his wagon, found it, and arrested him. The punishment for smuggling was death.

Yaacov walked with the police. After a few feet, he started walking a few steps ahead. Then, he began to run. They shot at his back, but he was fast, and they missed. He went home without the salami. That was his first near-death experience.

---

[6] A pointer used to keep place when reading the Torah scroll, which cannot be touched by bare hands

When he was a bit older, and his family's chance of survival looked slim, he and one of his brothers decided they were too much of a burden. They escaped into the forest, taking as much food as they could carry. This was a large forest, actually one of the biggest in the world. After a few days, Yaacov's brother said, "We'll never make it. I'm going back."

"You take the food. I'll keep going," Yaacov replied. After a few more days, he realized there was nowhere to go and returned home. His brother starved to death in the forest. Later, his body was found.

Yaacov wasn't able to leave Russia before he was drafted into the Russian army, which already, was openly anti-Semitic. But my great-grandfather was tough and athletic and bound to get into trouble. He was washing his clothes when a group of men approached him, making anti-Semitic comments. He fought them and beat them up. There were many larger, more dangerous battles, too. Once, he was bayonetted in the forehead.

His squad was sent on a mission that was clearly suicidal. Knowing they wouldn't survive, they decided to forfeit and face the consequences. After, they learned that the men of the other squads were killed on the mission. A few days later, a notice was posted requesting those who did not go on the mission to appear at a certain building. The notice promised security and understanding. Yaacov considered that he did not trust the Russians, so he didn't go. The other members of his squad were also killed.

Culture Shock

Eventually he too was caught and sent to a prison in a city in Siberia called Irkutsk, then known as the coldest city on earth. After a year as an inmate, the prison took note of his athleticism, and he became a trainer for new recruits. Thinking there must be more to life than the cold and drilling prisoners, he broke out of the prison, caught a train, jumped from it while it was still moving, and traveled three thousand miles through boreal forest until he reached the outskirts of Uzlian. As he walked through the town, two policemen recognized him. He ran from them to his parents' house, where he barged through the front door, starved and unrecognizable. With only the word of the man in front of her that he was her son, his mother hid him in a barn until the police passed. He didn't have much time. He got in touch with a cousin and started to make his way to the Polish front. At the border, he was shot at from both sides, but he made it across.

The police immediately pursued him, thinking he was a communist spy. He escaped and took shelter in a boarding house. He ate dinner quickly, retreated to his room, and slept. Early the next morning, while he was still sleeping, the police came to the boarding house, cleared out all the people, and surrounded the house. My great grandfather was awakened by the sound of bullhorns. "Rubenchick, come out!"

He came out with his hands raised. The police arrested him with the intention of sending him back to Russia. Sitting in prison, Yaacov thought. He knew there was one Jewish politician in the Polish government. Rare, but there was one. Yaacov wrote letters addressed to this man and dropped them from the window of his cell. He wasn't expecting anything, but it was the least he could do. As soon as he stepped foot in Russia, he would be killed. Of course, nothing happened. No order came for his release. No guards arrived to free him from his jail cell. He was boarding the truck to Russia, knowing he was going to die, when a soldier ran toward the truck. He panted, but composed himself to say, "Is there a Rubenchick here?"

The truck stopped and Yaacov's name was called. He got out and watched as the engine started and the truck headed for Russia. The letters had reached the politician. Yaacov signed up with the Jewish Zionist Organization to travel to Israel to be a pioneer. Instead, they sent him to a city about fifty miles west of Warsaw, called Lovitch. He was put up with the president of the local organization, Joseph Greenberg. Understandably, my great grandfather came to the Greenbergs' house looking wild, with his hair overgrown and his shoulder blades jutting from his back. He made a living teaching Hebrew and Torah to Joseph's daughter Sophie and her brothers, in exchange for food and a place to sleep. Despite the anti-Semitism in Poland, Sophie was allowed to attend school because she was outstandingly bright. She was smarter than everyone she knew until she met Yaacov. Every so often, the women of the town met at the Greenbergs' to discuss politics and literature. Sophie described how wild my great grandfather seemed. "I'd sooner die than marry a man like that."

As Yaacov and Sophie began to fall for each other, Yaacov failed to mention one small detail of his story: he was married. His first wife had been the pretty girl in town, the object of all the other men, but Yaccov won her hand. They had two daughters, Yentl and Shulamit. When he left Russia, he left alone.

Yaacov and Sophie were walking on a foggy day in the forest when police came through. Yaacov knew they would recognize him, so he told Sophie, "Don't worry. I'll be back" and escaped into the fog. Perhaps one person could only have so much luck. The police caught him and started to lead him forward. Yaacov knew what to do. He started to walk a little faster. Then he ran away. He returned to the Greenberg family. I imagine Sophie's face as Yaacov walked through the door. She cannot help her jaw from dropping. I imagine him hanging his coat on a hook, saying, "I told you I'd be back."

The Greenbergs traveled to Germany to catch a ship headed for America. Yaacov could not accompany them, because he was not in the Polish quota, so he found a ship that was taking people under the Polish and the Russian quotas. They were supposed to land in Boston. In the middle of the ocean, in the distance, they saw another refugee ship from Russia. Whichever ship arrived first would fill the Russian quota for refugees, and the Russian passengers on the second ship would be sent back. Yaacov's ship changed course to beat the other ship. The closest port was Portland, Maine. When they arrive, they saw the other ship already docked in the harbor.

As they waited for their fate to be decided, the passengers played pinochle. Yaacov had a photographic memory, so he was quite good at this game. So good, in fact, that he took other people's losing hands and helped them win. This drove one man in particular crazy. I imagine it went like this: Yaacov, this man, and their partners faced each other across a small wooden table illuminated only by the light that seeped through from tiny square windows. They were surrounded by the rest of the passengers, clumped together in the cramped space. One man, who was closer to the action, kept score on a small notebook with a pencil that was dangerously close to being too blunt to write with. Yaacov's opponent was sure he was winning as he lay down his cards. Yaacov lay down a trump card and won. His team won the game and another player slid in as Yaacov's partner. This continued until the two men were sworn enemies, and the State Department came aboard to interview the passengers. They asked Yaacov where he was from.

"Uzlian," he said.

"Where's that?" they asked.

He suddenly recalled the argument he'd had as a child. Uzlian really wasn't on the map. So Yaacov improvised. He said that if you looked out the window you could see a bigger town, which was on the border, but in Poland. In reality, if you looked out the window through seventy miles of forest, then you would see the town.

"What's the story?" His enemy asked as Yaacov returned from his interview.

"I have to go back," Yaacov said. After another waiting period, the State Department boarded the ship and read the list of people who could come ashore. They called out "Yaacov Rubenchick."

Yaacov waved goodbye to his Pinochle opponent. On land, they gave him a new name, "Rubin." In New York, 1923, he reunited with Sophie Greenberg and the classic American success story began.

Think back to that field in Belarus. Pogroms of rioters burned houses, pillaged fields and storehouses. In the 1940s, the Nazis came in, and all of Yaacov's brothers and sisters died in concentration camps.

There's a saying in my family that we eat like we won't see food in the next few days. This presents itself as only a slight untruth at our family dinners. As my zayde reaches for another drumstick, I see the shadow of my great grandfather arriving in the United States before the onset of the Great Depression, listening to Americans complaining about their lives. He never complained. He knew where he came from. Zayde tells me "A guy like that, when he comes to America, becomes the greatest patriot."

My Bubbe wipes her greasy hands on a napkin between bites, while my brother spoons soup mandels by the plateful, shovels rosemary potatoes into his mouth in a race to the last bite. My aunt takes nothing but diet coke, and my mother's stomach growls as she decides to skip dessert, which tonight, is pareve[7] babka from Seven Mile Market. Her grandfather Alexander from Austria watches hungrily. Around the dinner table, my eyesight blurs between past and present, and I wonder still what the odds are that we're all alive right now.

    On Yom Kippur, we starve and avoid each other's hungry gazes. We become our ancestors. We feel Siberian air clinging to us like a thin jacket. We escape bullets. We eat nothing but our fingernails.

    Twenty years after he first arrived, my great grandfather went to the State Department to tell them that he was actually Russian. They told him not to worry about it.

---

[7] Containing neither meat nor dairy

Some Jewish History: Abraham to Exodus

- In the seventeenth century BCE, a young man named Abram lives in Mesopotamia with his wife Sarai and his father. One night, a voice calls on him with the promises that his descendants will become a great nation. He can only trust that this voice is God. He leaves his home and travels to the land of Canaan.
- There's a slight problem with this promise: Sarai is barren and in her seventies. Instead, she offers him her handmaid Hagar. Hagar has a child, which makes Sarai so jealous that she drives Hagar away. So much for that plan. Pregnant Hagar is left wandering the desert. More about her later.
- The Covenant: "This is my covenant with you and your descendants after you, the covenant you are to keep: Every male among you shall be circumcised" (Genesis 17-10) Long story short: boys get circumcised at eight days old instead of ninety-nine years old, which is how old Abram is when he upholds his agreement. He becomes Abraham, "father of many," and his wife Sarai becomes Sarah, "mother of nations."

- As for God's end of the bargain, Sarah still doesn't have a child. Three angels visit Abraham's tent and tell him that Sarah will have a son in the next year. Sarah, who is listening in, can't help but laugh. She tries to deny laughing at all, but it's a bit difficult to keep anything from God. Sure enough, Sarah has a child, and names him Isaac, meaning laughter.
- Biblical flash forward: Isaac begets Jacob, and Jacob begets many sons, but Joseph is the important one. Joseph's brothers sell him to slavery in Egypt, and Joseph's psychic dreams lead him to become the Pharaoh's right-hand man.
- With a famine in Canaan, Joseph is reunited with his brothers, and the Israelites migrate to Egypt. By the thirteenth century BCE, the tables have turned, and all of the Jews are slaves in Egypt, building storehouses out of clay.
- A Jewish woman hides her baby son in a basket and floats him down a river. This isn't the safest way to give her child up for adoption, but luckily, the baby is rescued by the Pharaoh's daughter, who names him Moses, "to draw out." He grows up in royalty.
- When Moses is older, a burning bush tells him to take the Israelites out of Egypt.

Culture Shock

- Moses confronts Pharaoh and impresses with all sorts of magic tricks like turning his staff into a serpent and water into blood. Pharaoh stubbornly refuses to free the Israelites. Bad idea.
- God hits Egypt with the ten plagues:

1. Water turned to blood
2. Frogs
3. Lice
4. Wild animals
5. Pestilence
6. Boils
7. Thunderstorms of hail and fire
8. Locust invasion
9. Darkness for three days
10. Death of every Egyptian first born, including Pharaoh's

- At this point, Pharaoh learns his lesson and lets Moses lead the Israelites out of Egypt. The Israelites reach the Red Sea when Pharaoh changes his mind about letting them go. The Red Sea parts, the Israelites cross it, and the waves crash down again, drowning Egyptian soldiers, their chariots, and their horses.
- After worshipping golden calves, receiving the Torah, and being punished by God for forty years, the Israelites finally reach Israel.

Believing the Bible

When I was three years old, God spoke to me. I was crying over some silly thing a three year old cries about, maybe I had tripped, when a deep voice said, "Elana, stop crying." It was God, so I listened.

I had recently started preschool at the Jewish Community Center in the middle of the year because my family moved from New Jersey to Baltimore in December. When I came in my first day and put my butterfly roller backpack in the cubby, I saw that the other children already had best friends. Socially aware enough to know that I would become an outsider if I played alone, I joined two bossy girls who fought over Ritz crackers and dress up. When my mother picked me up, I complained that the other children wouldn't let me play with them. The teachers were confused when my mother called them, and the next class, they sent her pictures of me building blocks with the other kids.

In class, the teacher asked if God had ever spoken to one of us. I crawled out of the corner to raise my hand. "He spoke to me," I said. "He told me to stop

Culture Shock

crying." I can't remember the look on the teacher's face, but she went along with it. A year later, when I reminded my father of the story, I still believed God had spoken to me. My father laughed and cupped his hands over his mouth, speaking in the deep voice I had heard. God was as silent as he'd been for thousands of years; it was my father all along. He was surprised I remembered.

Of course I remembered. We learned about Abraham and the covenant, and then Moses and the burning bush. Of all history, of all the places in the world, they were the chosen ones. I knew what it meant to have your name called out.

I never approached Judaism with quite the same interest. Bible stories, with their miracles and supernatural punishments, were exciting to learn, but didn't have much to do with my life. The next year, I started preschool at the early childhood education center at my synagogue. As in any preschool, we learned to spell, add and subtract, and express ourselves "using our words." We played "house" and went to the playground to mount the dinosaur climber, which I was too scared to climb, and ride the Merry-Go-Cycle, pedaling around a circle. Once, a friend and I were at the reading station, listening to *The Little Mermaid* on a cassette tape, looking at the pictures in our laps. When the narrator said, "And they lived happily ever after," and we closed the book and took our headphones out, the room was empty. The teacher, who had been waiting for us, took us to the lobby where our class was driving Little Tikes Cozy Coupes.

Unlike other preschools, we were immersed entirely in Hebrew for half the day. Every Friday, a different girl wore a daisy crown and brought her parents into class for a Shabbat celebration. In kindergarten, we learned to write our ABCs along with the Hebrew alphabet. We baked elephant ears and monkey bread while coloring pictures of Adam and Eve in the Garden of Eden. One art project was decorating challah[1] covers, and on Passover, we painted our own seder plates to bring home. In first grade, we were given our first Bible books in simplified Hebrew, small and blue, with a cartoon drawing of Abraham on the front. I brought it home for my mother to laminate.

My family practiced Judaism moderately. On Shabbat, we turned the lights on and drove. My sister and I wore shorts and whispered to each other during prayer. Still, we kept kosher. At Jewish day school, we learned the blessings over the candles and grape juice, which we recited every Friday night. We sang the old versions in Hebrew because my father was frustrated with Reform Judaism and said the sing-songy version, "Hamotzi Lechem Min Haaretz, we give thanks to God for bread…," which I had learned in preschool and

---

[1] A fluffy braided bread eaten on Shabbat and some Jewish holidays; makes delicious French toast

Culture Shock

Jewish day camp, wasn't a real blessing. Occasionally, we went to synagogue.

I thought of the Bible as truth because I didn't know any differently, and I liked reading from our Bible book because my class was learning to read Hebrew at the same time. In first grade, I was used to feeling stupid. I was in the lowest math class, and since I didn't like math, or the feeling of the rug beneath me as we sat around the teacher's chair, I traced the inside cover of my workbook, which had the impression of a dog. Eventually, we were banned from opening our workbooks, which made learning math quite difficult.

I was so bad at reading that a few other students and I were in a special class beneath the lowest level. I practiced reading *Junie B. Jones* aloud to my mother on the couch. After struggling through three pages in maybe twenty minutes, my mom suggested we take a break and start another time.

Eventually, the letters began to fit together in a way that made sense. I recognized patterns. My teacher assigned me more advanced books than the other girls in my special group, and I read them rapidly to show how fluent I had become, or maybe to make up for the six years I could not read. In second grade, when I was reading everything I could get my hands on, we began to read the actual words of the Bible. In a zig-zag pattern around our desks, each of us stumbled through a line, as the teacher waited painfully for us to complete a passage, before spending the rest of class explaining what it meant. The story was exciting for the first few days, until we realized we were reading the same thing over and over. We probably read Genesis a dozen times before fourth grade, when we started Exodus.

I waited two years for the Israelites to reach Israel, as one would wait for the season finale of a television show. I waited as they worshiped the golden calf, and as they received the Torah on Mount Sinai. Their arrival was somewhat underwhelming. Spies returned and spoke of giants roaming the land. The Israelites were frightened and did not see how they could defeat the Canaanites. For this, they were punished and forced to wander through the desert for forty years, which was enough time for the unbelieving generation to die off.

I waited tearfully as Moses died, seeing the Promised Land all around him, but not allowed to touch it.[2] Finally, the Israelites crossed the Jordan River, carrying the Ark of the Covenant. The Israelites were instructed to decimate and burn down the city of Jericho but not to plunder. However, a soldier named Achan took treasure, causing the Israelites' defeat in the city of Ai and the death of thirty six-soldiers. Achan confessed, and he and his children were stoned to death and burned with all their possessions. Bible stories were not as simple as I had thought. I could see

---

[2] This was Moses's punishment for hitting a rock to draw water when God told him to talk to it. See Numbers 20:8

why the school had waited so long to teach us the actual text.

This was the year we also started to learn Jewish history, including an extensive Holocaust unit, which made me too sick to eat my lunch. I could not understand why God was so concerned with making sure the Jews didn't worship idols but was nowhere to be found when six million of them were murdered in gas chambers and concentration camps. That year, our teachers told us that the Bible should be loosely interpreted. The book was approached with more questioning, more acknowledgement of the supernatural that could not actually exist. The teacher explained that before the world was created, there was only *tohu va bohu.*

"Swirling masses of nothingness," the teacher said.

"But what is that?" someone asked.

"Nothing," the teacher said. "There was actually nothing."

I opened the palm of my hand. My hand was not empty. I was holding air and germs and dust particles. In fourth grade, I was in the highest reading group. When we finished our classwork, we were allowed to take a book from the back of the room. I rushed through math problems, reading questions, and spelling and raced to the back of the room to claim my book, *The Time Machine* by H. G. Wells. After stealing fifteen minutes at a time over a few weeks, I finished it. When the time traveler didn't return, I avoided the sinking feeling in my stomach by standing quietly, returning the book to its shelf, and asking to use the bathroom.

My best friend and I read *The Unicorn Chronicles* by Bruce Coville. We decided to go to the world of the unicorns. I took a piece of white hair that my dog had shed and placed it inside a locket. At recess, we held hands, counted to ten, and jumped off the bleachers. We opened our eyes, disappointed we were still on the field. A teacher told us to stop because she was scared we would hurt ourselves. My other friend called me crazy for believing in unicorns. After school, I tried it by myself, opened my eyes, and found myself grabbing fistfuls of grass from the field. After a few days, I dropped the grass in frustration and never jumped off the bleachers again.

This was the year I spent my bedtime trying to make sense of the world instead of sleeping. I imagined building a time machine by capturing stars, which could carry us light years away. I wondered if time existed on a timeline or all at once, like in the book I was reading, *When You Reach Me*, or if it was a combination of strings, like in *A Wrinkle in Time*. I understood how trees grew and how the earth turned and why space was dark and there was no gravity, but I always got stuck in the same place: How could the universe be infinite? Eventually, I had to settle with knowing that there were parts of the world I would never understand because the human mind was only capable of comprehending so much.

Culture Shock

    I gave up writing letters to my tooth fairy to prove she existed. I stopped waiting for the supernatural creature (I thought it must be a dragon egg or a fairy, if not a unicorn) that I was meant to discover to reveal itself to me. No voice was going to call me in the middle of the night.

After we read about the Red Sea drowning Pharaoh's army, our teacher showed us a video of a diver exploring a coral reef. Buried in the sand was a chariot wheel and jewels, proof that the Egyptians really had attempted to cross the Red Sea. I believed it. My parents told me it was impossible. Even if chariots really had drowned, the wheels would have disintegrated by now. I thought about it and realized they were probably right. I was tired and a little heartbroken by false hope. Along with books on time travel and unicorns, it was time to put the Bible aside, to save it for when I needed a good story.

Family Heirlooms

In preparation for my Bat Mitzvah, my parents and I met with the cantor of our synagogue. He had me flip through a calendar that listed historical events for every day of every year until I came to the day of my birth. On March 20th, 1999, *Burn Hollywood Burn* won the Golden Raspberry Award, British painter Patrick Heron died, and a Swiss hot air balloon won a record for circumnavigating the world in nineteen days. The cantor said that coincidences did not exist but were acts of God. Perhaps the events that occurred simultaneously with my birth explain my appreciation for theater, the arts, and moving at a fast pace. We like to believe that coincidences serve a greater purpose, that our lives follow some larger plan, that the patterns in our lives have meaning. In the end, we don't really know why coincidences happen. Perhaps they serve as a reminder that life is hard and you shouldn't take it too seriously. Anyway, they make for some interesting story telling.

    My great grandfather wasn't the only one in his family who sought a new life in America. In the

Culture Shock

1880s, my great-great-great grandfather, whose name is unknown, left Uzlian alone and found a job in the United States. He returned to Minsk to bring his family to America, but his wife refused, tied to the tradition of the shtetl. The rabbis discouraged people from leaving the Pale of Settlement for "godless" America. It was hard to make a living in Russia, so he came back to America alone and is now buried somewhere in Brooklyn.

In the 1890s, my great-great-grandfather, Mordechai Rubenchick, came to New York, lived in a tenement home, and worked as a house painter. He returned to Russia and tried to persuade his family to join him, and they also refused. So they stayed in Russia, where Yaacov Rubenchick grew up and became the first in his family to leave for good.

Arriving in Brooklyn at the onset of the farm depression in the 1920s, with the skills of a Hebrew teacher and no knowledge of English, Yaacov had to work to survive. Like his father before him, Yaacov became a house painter. He also drove a jitney with a little register and coins. He opened the backdoor by pulling a lever in the front, so the customers didn't have to open the door to get in. Speaking no English, he drove in silence. They paid him, without looking at him, and he gave back change. He also owned a parking lot.

These jobs were a waste of his mind. When a rabbi had trouble understanding a difficult section of Gemara, Yaacov stood before him and quoted the

Mishnah, then the Gemara, and then Rashi. The rabbi had not seen anything like that in forty years. Yaacov knew Hebrew better than his native language of Yiddish. He was intrigued by Hamlet's soliloquy, but could not recite it because of his accent. "Toe beh, or not toe beh," he said. He studied English and algebra, took state exams, and scored one hundred percent on all of them.

He once had a disagreement with a great scholar and a journalist of Judaism at the top of his field. Yaacov noted that the journalist was misquoting in his argument. His guests suggested they take a look at the book.

"We've been doing this for many years," Yaacov said, "Have I ever been wrong?"

"You've never been wrong," the journalist admitted. "Let's check anyway." Of course, Yaacov was right. He had a photographic memory.

Taking more teaching and tutoring jobs, he was able to make just enough money to survive. Then, he hurt his finger on a job and received a medical settlement of three thousand dollars. For the first time in his life, he was rich. He and his friends decided to buy a hotel. At the last minute, Yaacov became fearful of the debt and responsibility of taking a mortgage. He withdrew from the plan and bought a house instead for cash with no mortgage. The hotel became a multi-million dollar business. It's called Teplitzky's, one of the most popular hotels in Atlantic City.

Culture Shock

In a kitchen cabinet, my mother keeps a vase and salt box that her grandmother, Henrietta Wolok, bought from a flea market. In our living room, she displays china, a fireplace kindling box, and a silver-plated tea set, also from her grandmother. On the bookshelf are my father's *machzors*[1], given to him by his father, who received them from his father. In Judaism, we cherish the same objects that our ancestors cherished. It is how we keep their memories alive.

One year, my great grandparents hosted Passover for a group of people from a facility, where they were recovering from accidents and trauma. After the meal was over, my great grandfather drove them home. Normally driving a little too fast, he drove at a slow pace so they wouldn't feel nervous. Despite his image as a tough man who emphasized discipline, my great grandfather believed that everyone should have a place to go for Pesach.

Compassion is never a coincidence. Through generations of parents teaching their children, values become treasured family heirlooms. Rather than fate or the day of my birth, my artistic and musical interests most likely come from my great grandfather, who learned the clarinet, violin, and mandolin and played until he hurt his fingers and got his insurance money. His sons bought him a mandolin for his birthday forty years later, and he could still hold down the strings even though he lost feeling in two of his

---

[1] Prayer books for the high holy days

fingers. He had a lovely voice and won a singing contest for knowing the most Yiddish songs. He wrote poems to my great grandmother and sent them on postcards.

My great grandparents first stayed in an apartment in the back of a butcher shop. They had their first son, Emanuel, or Manny, in 1928, six months before the stock market crashed. The next year, they had another son, Mordechai, or Moe. At one point, Yaacov had one dime left, and he and Sophie sat down to decide what to do with it. They took a walk, bought two ice cream cones, and sat silently eating them on a park bench. Eventually, there were five boys: Manny, Moe, Asher, Joseph (Yussel), and Abba. When the family had six dollars, they decided to go out for steaks.

Abba Rubin's first memory is as a toddler, standing in his crib and crying because his grandmother was in the same room, and she was ill. His parents heard him and came to take care of her. Abba recalls bits and pieces of Atlantic City. When he was five or so, he was sent to his father's parking lot and was terrified of the rushing cars, afraid they wouldn't see him because he was so little. He remembered sitting on the handlebars of Moe's bicycle when Moe took him to day camp. His mother gave him the biggest compliment he'd ever received. "Children are brutish animals, all of them, except Abba." When he was six, his parents sent him to a yeshiva.

Culture Shock

When Abba was almost seven, his parents took their children on vacation in Liberty, New York. There, his father met a doctor, who was so impressed with him, he immediately offered him a job teaching Hebrew. Yaacov had been tutoring for bar mitzvahs and still managed his parking lot, which made some money, but this was a better deal. They moved to Liberty, where Yaacov began teaching six-year-olds how to read Hebrew, sing Hebrew songs, and celebrate Jewish holidays.

Winters in Liberty were brutal. Abba and his brothers walked to school in the cold and through the snow. Their mother baked them potatoes to keep in their pockets so their hands wouldn't get cold. Like his father, Abba was fairly strong. There were a couple of kids, including a bully who had been held back a few years, who liked to pick on Jews, but they never messed with Abba.

At night, Abba's mother turned the lights on and found cockroaches covering the floor. The children slept in a tiny room. When they wanted to hear a story, their father translated a Hebrew book into Yiddish because they didn't know Hebrew yet. On one side of the room was Asher's bed, and on the other side, with a small path between, Yussel and Abba shared a double bed. Abba slept on the far side, so he had to climb over his brother to sleep. Sometimes they played together and made noises at night. In the other room, their father said, "Be quiet." This scared them.

When their father told them to get quiet, they immediately got quiet.

One night, Yussel and Abba switched places. Yussel began to make noises and Abba begged him to stop. He did not stop, and their father came in after a number of warnings. Usually, he hit whoever was closest to him, which would have been Yussel on any other night. However, Yussel had switched sides. He was making noises so that his brother could get a turn. They heard their father's footsteps approach the bed and heard him say, "It's about time the other one gets it." He reached across Abba, who trembled beneath his arm, and hit Yussel a few times. Yussel cried heavily, and their father left the room. Abba was panting, but safe. About thirty years later, it dawned on him that his father must have known that Yussel was making the noise.

When Abba was in fourth grade, sitting in class with a friend, his father stopped by to see how he was doing. When Abba saw his father through the window, he thought he might have a heart attack. He wondered what he'd done wrong. The teacher opened the door and they spoke. His father asked how Abba was doing.

"Fine," the teacher responded. "But his friend is giving me some trouble." Yaacov took Abba's friend out to the hallway for a chat. For the next two weeks, the friend sat straight up in class, petrified.

Sophie taught too. When one of the children misbehaved, she told them, "I have to go make dinner for Mr. Rubin, so you'll have to sit in his class." They all immediately came to attention and turned to their books.

At the same time, the school children loved him. They kissed their teacher before leaving for home. When they happened to catch sight of him downtown, they approached him and said, "Shalom, Mr. Rubin!" and ran around the block to say it again. It was the same kind of feeling his children had for him. They loved him and respected him, but they also feared him. In Judaism, that's what God is supposed to do for you.

Yaacov also taught at Livingston Manor, which was seven miles higher in elevation than Liberty, one of the highest towns in the Catskill Mountains. The weather was always bad, and in the winter, the roads were full of snow and ice. On a particularly ruthless day, Yaacov was driving home inch by inch on the edge of a cliff, stopping to check where the road was. He drove over a patch of black ice, and the car spun around and fell over the cliff. The car jolted against rock, knocking Yaacov into the back seat. Another bang knocked the steering wheel into the front seat. Halfway down, the car hit a tree and stopped. Yaacov got out of the car and climbed to the top of the cliff, where a crowd had formed and people were beginning to descend to help him. Yaacov broke his shoulder blade, but beside that, he was fine.

Abba has no explanation for what occurred next. That afternoon, his mother was sleeping in her bed. Suddenly, she sat up and screamed, "Daddy had an accident." A few minutes later, the call came that Yaacov was in the hospital, where he stayed for two and a half weeks. Abba doesn't know how his mother knew. She never experienced anything like that again.

Abba starred in every school play from first grade until he graduated. In high school, he was a member of the National Thespian Society and wrote plays for his school to put on. He traveled across the state with his debate team, attending tri-state tournaments and winning every speech contest that he entered. He claims he wasn't always a good debater. He couldn't easily win against poor competition without his partner. But against a tough team, he told his partner to be quiet while he quickly developed a theory of economics. Research consisted of asking his father about the topics, "Dad, if you were for this, what would you say? If you were against it, what would you say?" When the other team brought up a quotation to prove a point, Abba stood up and said, "It isn't who said it that matters but why they said it. If you want to be persuasive, tell us why they said it. I will tell you why it doesn't work." This argument allowed him to avoid doing research.

Abba's high school created a position "Class Orator" so he could give a speech at graduation. At the same time, Abba was elected to a statewide student Congress as the Senator from New York in the National Student Congress in Florida. He missed his graduation and the school did away with the position.

Culture Shock

In Florida, he was elected "superior speaker." He enjoyed pulling a "shtick."[2] While his competitors went to the front of the room to speak, Abba would stand up and speak from his seat. In the last speech, he walked to the front. Whispers trailed the aisle, "He's going to the front of room! Why is he going to the front of the room?" He reached the podium, surveyed the audience with an intense stare, and said, "I just wanted to see the faces of those people who…" and then made his argument.

Abba was not tough like his father, but he was when he had to be. After college, he became a teacher and accidentally broke a kid's hand. In another case, a little kid was walking down the hallway, making noise, and disrupting his class. Abba went out to the hallway and yelled at the kid. When he refused to stop making noise, Abba picked him up, slammed him against the lockers, and told the kid to behave around him. He calmed down and put the kid back on the ground. The kid walked away. Afterward, every time Abba passed him in the hall, the kid said, "Hi, Mr. Rubin."

What Abba didn't know was that this kid's father and brothers were gangsters. Whenever people bothered this kid, his father and brothers broke their arms and legs or killed them. Instead of sending the gang after Abba, the kid began to respect him. No teacher had ever dared to discipline him before.

---

[2] Yiddish for a gimmick

Memories are heirlooms too. Many years later, Abba traveled out west to visit a friend from high school. Only the friend's wife knew he was visiting. When Abba knocked on the door, she opened it, and the friend, who was an accountant, was sitting in the kitchen, helping his daughter with math.

"No, I think this…" he was saying when he saw Abba. He fell off his chair.

Abba and his friend still correspond occasionally, he told me as I sat across from him in the living room. Abba attended most of his high school reunions. He enjoyed seeing people, but he was also saddened by the people who had died. He took a minute to think. He was sitting in his armchair, wearing a blue polo shirt with a notebook in the front pocket. Across the room on an end table is a framed portrait of his father. On a wooden shelf beside the piano, next to the pictures that his children drew when they were in high school, are faded pictures of Bubbe's parents, Bubbe with Yaacov and Sophie, Abba and his brothers. On the same shelf, like a patchwork of old and new, sit colored photos of my cousins as babies, my siblings and I posing in bright clothing.

"It's funny," he said. "You're uncovering all these memories I haven't thought about in years."

SJH: King Saul to Persian Empire

- In 1046 BCE, the Jewish Monarchy is led by its first king, Saul. God instructs King Saul to decimate the evil Amalekites. Saul destroys everyone and everything except King Agag and the best sheep and cattle. Frustrated by disobedience, yet again, God rejects Saul as the King of Israel.
- The prophet Samuel travels to Bethlehem and anoints the shepherd David as the next king. The Philistines, who are at war with Israel, send a giant warrior, Goliath. David is able to kill the giant with a slingshot.
- Saul becomes jealous of David and tries to kill him. Luckily, David escapes and eventually becomes king.
- David defeats the Philistines, Moab, and Syrians, establishing his kingdom as the major power in the Middle East. He conducts foreign affairs and makes friendly alliances with surrounding kingdoms. His son Absalom tries to overthrow him, but David is pretty good at staying alive.

- David's hands are bloody with war, so the task of building the first temple is given to his son, Solomon, who becomes a symbol of peace. When David dies, Solomon becomes king and builds a temple in Jerusalem, where the tabernacle is finally laid to rest.
- After Solomon dies, the land is split into Judah, where the tribes descendent of Judah and Benjamin reside, and Israel, where the ten northern tribes live.
- The Assyrians seize Israel and the tribes are exiled. Babylonia conquers Judah, destroying Jerusalem and the temple. The Jews are exiled and end up getting dispersed around the globe (AKA the Jewish Diaspora).
- In 539 BCE, the Persians vanquish the Babylonians, seize Mesopotamia, and allow Jews to return to Judea. The Jews rebuild the temple in Jerusalem.

Everything Under the Sun

One of the first stories Jewish children learn involves two prostitutes and the dismembering of an infant. The women come to King Solomon, frantic, both claiming a single baby as their own. They live in the same house, and their babies were born three days apart. One of the babies died, and each accuses the other of replacing her dead baby with the other's living baby. King Solomon takes the baby and orders his servants to bring him a sword. It is only fair that he cuts the baby in half, and each woman can have half a baby. The first woman insists that the other woman take the baby. The second woman tells Solomon to cut the baby in half so neither would get the baby. Solomon gives the baby to the first woman.

In fifth grade Bible class, we read Kohelet, traditionally attributed to King Solomon:

> "Utter futility?—said Kohelet—
> "Utter futility! All is futile!
> What real value is there for a man
> In all the gains he makes under the
> sun?" (Kohelet 1:2-4).

My teacher told us how this passage discouraged her. Solomon, one of the wisest, most accomplished scholars, believed that life was long and monotonous with nothing new and nothing meaningful. In the end, all of her life, all the work my teacher had done, meant nothing.

I imagined Solomon was depressed. He became famous for knowing "everything," but his studies led him to nothing. As Hemingway once said, "Happiness in intelligent people is the rarest thing I know."

I felt a connection to Solomon that I had not to other Biblical figures. I realized I was lonely in kindergarten. Sometimes during recess, when I thought my friends liked each other more than they liked me, I sat on the playset, on the damp wooden steps leading to the slide, singing to myself. They were usually the sad songs from *The Ugly Duckling*.

I was preoccupied with solitary activities. Besides watching *The Ugly Duckling* on repeat, I sat at tables by myself, drawing. In my earliest memories, I asked my mother to copy pictures from my favorite books, *The Little Mermaid* and *Beauty and the Beast*. I began to copy them myself. Soon I was drawing without a guide, scrawling what I saw in my mind, dolls and fairies and giant butterflies with multi-colored wings. I drew a duck that was so impressive, my preschool teacher hung it up on the wall outside the classroom.

Culture Shock

My mother decided it was time to find a private art teacher. She and the mother of a girl from my class took us to trial classes of many different teachers. The girl was blonde and had cracked her head open on a staircase. She scared me, and she didn't like any of the teachers. We tried a red haired woman who lived in a cluttered home and another who taught us how to make stepping stones from concrete. After a few more rejections by the blonde girl and a couple watercolor paintings later, we took a lesson from the mother of one of our classmates, who taught us how to paint a rose. We both liked her, but somehow, the plan fell through. Eventually, my mother decided that art camp was good enough.

During the summers, I learned how to make pottery and sculptures, how to draw from "the right side of the brain," how to paint and how to shade charcoal. In school, I developed a love for Language Arts. On the last day of first grade, my teachers presented each of us a journal. I began to write almost daily. When I reached the last page, I bought another, and when I filled that one, yet another. Eventually, I amassed five personal journals, along with journals for writing, planning, secret codes, and revision.

In third grade, my teacher was Mrs. Goldstein. Every week, she gave us writing prompts, and we had to write stories. I wrote one about a dog who became friends with a flea on his back. There was another about a magical potion. For Mrs. Goldstein's birthday, I wrote a book in verse called *Have you ever Looked up at a Hill?* with illustrated pictures. Proud of my work, I made a copy for myself and redrew all of the images. Along with a package of Godiva chocolate, I put this book in a shiny red bag, which I kept in my locker for a week because I was embarrassed to give it to her. The day she received the gift, she gave me a thank you note with a red rose lollipop, which I didn't eat for a year because it was so beautiful.

In fifth grade, Mrs. Simon was our writing workshop teacher. I entered the classroom, sat down at a computer, began to type, and was transported far away. I wrote about genies and travel through time and space. I wrote about dream pills that cured nightmares. I wrote about the time I saved my dog during a thunderstorm because he was stuck in the woods. I wrote about my Polish babysitter leaving the country without saying goodbye. The bell would ring, and I would feel the stiff chair beneath me and the keys glossy beneath my fingers. I rose, slung my backpack over my shoulder, and found my next class in a daze.

The summer before eighth grade, my art teachers reviewed my sketches and told me I had potential. They encouraged me to audition for a magnet art school. I found a group of friends to sit with at lunch. In the afternoon, we giggled and told each other stories as we worked with clay. One afternoon, I left our lunch table to fill my water bottle. When I returned, the table was empty. My sister walked over from her lunch group to tell me that she heard them say "Quick! Get out before she comes back!"

I looked outside. They were playing hopscotch. I went to the art bin, picked up a pencil and a piece of paper and sketched until it was time for sculpture class. By eighth grade, I realized it was stupid to try and make friends. I was meant to be alone and lie awake every night, wondering about the purpose of life and if the universe was actually infinite.

A few weeks before seventh grade, I got glasses. I had needed them since fourth grade, but fear of looking ugly and confirming my status as a nerd delayed the inevitable, until I needed to sit in the first row to read the board. At first, I gasped at the details I saw for the first time. I could read every sign on the highway. I did not know that it was possible to see the individual leaves on trees. However, when school began, I didn't like the way they looked and put them on only when I needed to see the board.

I had terrible anxiety over getting a B instead of an A in a class. I wouldn't wear a skirt because everyone else wore one, so I wore pants and worried that I looked frumpy. Knowing that I was not as smart as my reputation suggested I was, I did not participate in class so I could never be wrong. If I was shy in elementary school, I was a recluse in middle school. I could make myself invisible in a classroom if I tried hard enough. I wrote stories in composition notebooks. I realized I was the only one who still wrote.

On the first day seventh grade, my Language Arts teacher, Ms. Platzke, shook my hand as I hid behind my glasses. Other teachers let me slip into class and out of class unnoticed, but she saw something in me that I didn't see in myself. I don't know what it was, but she looked at me in amazement as I turned *The Night Thoreau Spent in Jail* into a medieval play starring my eight-year-old siblings.

In eighth grade, tired of sitting through lunch as my peers chatted around me, I began to eat lunch against the locker. In Language Arts, we read *Romeo and Juliet*. I loved it: the cadence, the words, the heartbreaking irony that convinced my class that critics had mistaken it for a tragedy when it was really a comedy. I gave a fifteen minute presentation on Shakespeare having a mental illness based on his characters in *Romeo and Juliet* and *Hamlet*. I offered that his death could have been a suicide.

As I walked to my seat, a boy said, "Yeah, he was definitely crazy." It was nice to hear validation. I decided to apply to that magnet art school, but for writing. Ms. Platzke lent me poetry books to prepare for my audition. Now I had something to do while I ate lunch against my locker. I like to say that I first experienced love there in the muted hallway, reading "To a Waterfowl." Soon, I moved into her classroom, as she gave up lunches to talk to me about books: *Of Mice and Men*, *To Kill a Mockingbird*, *Percy Jackson*. I wrote fiction, poems, analyses, and informative essays and gave them to her. I had never let someone read my

Culture Shock

work before. There was a short story about a piano protégé, who did not hear the applause, but only felt the music still pounding through her fingertips at the end of the performance. Ms. Platzke told me that the story made her cry, "I see so much of you in this." I can never know what it was that she saw, but I'm glad she saw it. I got into the school and told her I was going to be a writer.

Every year during Yom Kippur, when there was nothing to do but sit in services or wander the hallways, I followed a staircase with velvet cloth leading up to a museum entrance with a sunset painted on the walls. In the middle of the soft golden clouds was a door handle, which opened to the fifth grade lockers.

I walked through the hallway, marveling that I was taller than the tops of the lockers, which were impossible to reach in fifth grade. I passed the water fountains, the bathrooms next to the basement entrance, which I took to get to my woodworking elective. There were the Language Arts classrooms, running parallel to the Hebrew rooms on the other side of the locker hallway. If I continued walking, I passed the lounge, the office, the library, until I faced the hallway to the upstairs elementary school classrooms— second to fourth grade. The same perfume smell of the carpets from my elementary school days is still present in that hallway. I call it the smell of the past.

Later I learned that Kohelet wasn't as pessimistic as I thought. Because life is transitory, Solomon meant that I should be happy and "make gardens and orchards," to laugh and "not to deprive the heart of joy."

From this I developed a life philosophy: If I mess up my life completely, it doesn't matter, because we all die anyway. My friends called me crazy for it. After reading *Man's Search for Meaning* by Viktor E. Frankl, I amended the motto. Life was short, so it must hold absolute meaning. The meaning of life is to find purpose, one that will keep me alive even after I die. If what I write connects with just one person now and another a hundred years from now, my life will have been deliberate.

When I was sixteen, I found that purpose. I was convinced that art, poetry especially, evoked emotions that were necessary for fulfillment. I visited Ms. Platzke and taught her seventh grade class how imagery was used to make poetry concrete and relatable. I taught them how to read poetry aloud, slowly and with confidence. I watched their eyes light up as they recited selected poems to the their class. I went to my public library and asked to start a poetry program for middle school students. Only one girl kept coming back to the meeting room every month.

"Voice is the fingerprint of an author," I explained to her, as I clicked the next PowerPoint slide on my laptop. She sorted through the murder mystery game I created, where she was instructed to assign poems to their authors using "criminal profiles," or background information. She confidently matched "Aunt Jennifer's Tigers" with Samuel Taylor Coleridge. I gently explained that Adrienne Rich was born nearly two hundred years after Coleridge.

Eventually, I opened up the session for all ages. In the last meeting, four adults attended. One woman brought her ninety-nine year old mother, who had never written a poem. I watched them facing me, bent over pages, thinking, shocked even. They were children again, and the world was bright, like the first time I read a poem there in the cold middle school hallway and felt my heartbeat to its rhythm.

Last Yom Kippur, I ran into Mrs. Goldstein. Her commanding presence has transformed into a sweet old lady, who is quite a few inches shorter than me, with the same jet black hair she'd had when I was in third grade. She asked how my poetry group was going, and I told her we were starting sessions again in January. I talked about the colleges I was applying to. I asked how she was doing, and she responded with the usual pleasantries. I left wondering how school teachers can bear it.

Year after year, they teach the same inquisitive students with large eyes. They take Band-Aids from their desks for students who trip on the playground, and they wipe away their tears. They answer the same questions: What is infinite? How do birds fly? Why is the moon out during the day?, over and over with the same cheerfulness. How can they watch them year after year, growing older, taller, fuller until they're adults towering over them? How can they watch them lose that spark that they had when they loved to learn? How can they let them watch the news and see politicians yelling for uprisings and children coughing, covered in rubble and mud? Perhaps the most important job of a teacher is to impart knowledge and let be. To watch their students gather it up and do with it as they please.

Maybe teachers never will be paid enough, or maybe they'll end up feeling worthless like Solomon. But we'll never know what they really think, the words they don't let slip. They leave their problems at the door and move into a different role as they enter the classroom. They arrange desks, clean off crumbs, stack papers and greet every child as he or she enters the room. I cannot thank my teachers for what these simple gestures and routines have done for me. The least I can do is immortalize them on this page.

The Fight

This is the kind of thing you write closing the computer as people walk past because you don't want them to read it. That is to say, this is going to be awkward. I knew it was going to be awkward when I started writing it, but I'm writing it anyway. Because it's important.

    I can't really remember when it all started, this perfection thing. In kindergarten, I got tired of being alone and decided that to stop being by myself, I had to stop being myself. Some days I pretended to be a boy named Josh, distracting myself by copying the way the boys walked with their legs farther apart. I started picking a new person every few months, copying the mannerisms that made people like them and critiquing mine that made them not want me. Maybe that's when it started.

    When I was going into fourth grade, I was probably as imperfect as I could get. I was a tomboy with short hair, who wore basketball shorts and shoes from the boys' section. I also had an imaginary pet squirrel, who I watched jump over shadows on the highway. I attended a summer day camp called Camp Holiday. Every morning, I waited by the end of my driveway until the bus pulled up. Then, I evaded the counselors and found a seat in the back, but not too far back, because that's where the loud kids with lots of friends sat. I placed my backpack on my lap, and the combined weight of the towel, brown bag lunch, and change of clothes made it feel warm and alive. I imagined it was my pet and held it to my chest when it rained and everyone else on the bus covered themselves with their towels because we couldn't figure out how to close the bus windows.

I'm trying to "show" myself being strange. Or is this just unnecessary exposition?

Sometimes, I sat next to a girl from my ~~cabin~~ bunk. I can't remember much about her except that her face was covered with freckles and she was forced to play a monkey in her school's production of "Horton Hears a Who." She asked me questions about *The Secret Garden*, while I gushed on about Mary and Collin and Dustin and the key and the garden enclosed in the wall, thinking she was just as passionate about the book as I was. She thanked me for completing her summer reading for her and chuckled in triumph. I felt stupid for a long time after that.

I'm so embarrassed. Martha's brother, who rescues orphan animals, his name is Dickon. I'm a complete literature fraud.

Fourth grade me can be described as "shy," or maybe "bookworm.

Culture Shock

And now I'm "telling."

In half the pictures my dad has taken of me, I'm curled up with a thick book, smiling at the camera with a faraway look in my eye. I'm in a different world. The girls at Camp Holiday weren't shy or bookworms. They were "popular" and "girly girls."

Weak descriptions, my writing should be more elevated than this.

With my basketball shorts and boy shoes, I was the weirdo of the bunk.

Really "telling" now.

I made friends: tall girls with glasses, or overweight girls with red hair, people who didn't fit in with the tan, skinny girls with long, glossy ponytails. They wouldn't speak to me. They left me in the locker room before swim, and I came out into the sunlight feeling embarrassed, fat in my orange tankini, as they stood outside the pool in their bikinis, spraying themselves with sunscreen, and ignoring me as I joined them.

My perspective is too self-centered. In their defense, I was really weird.

Once in the locker room, when I was trying to hurry so they wouldn't leave me behind, one of the girls approached me. She gave me a disgusted look. I will never forget that look, like I was a piece of gum stuck to her shoe.

Cliché.

"Why do you keep following us?" she said.

"What?" I asked.

"I said," her voice turned threatening, "Why do you keep following us?"

The tall girl with glasses stood between us. "She's kind of part of this bunk, duh," she said. I thanked her silently with my eyes and forced myself not to cry.

I was too sensitive.

You might be happy to know that Camp Holiday has since been shut down. The founders found themselves in financial trouble and could not afford to keep it running.

I can't help but smirk when I write that. I'm trying to make my writing sound like a smirk, but nothing ever comes out the way I want it to.

I tried to forget about the summer. But the following year, I wanted long red hair with green eyes and freckles. I was tan, with cropped brown hair. I was starting to develop acne before any of my classmates. I remember looking out the window with one of my classmates on a rainy day filled with deep gray clouds.

"I love rainy days." I sighed.

"It feels miserable," my classmate said.

"But don't you like feeling miserable sometimes?" I asked.

"No?" he said. I turned back to the window.

But, who says things like that?

In middle school, I returned from Israel and found that I had become the metaphor I had imagined for myself: "the tree in the middle of a building," out of place and unwanted. My best friends had already added a fourth member to our group to replace me while I was gone. On a trip to Hershey Park, they chose each other and left me behind.

Because I told them that I didn't like roller coasters. I overreacted.

Realizing that I was getting a belly, I learned how to count my calories. I often locked myself in my room on weekends, until three, to avoid eating. Eventually, I would stuff myself and gain back all the weight in Goldfish and bread. I decided it was time to change again. Maybe that's when it started.

When I came home from school, I stared at myself in the mirror, poking at my stomach, which didn't actually exist, but I saw it like a giant balloon.

I was a little chubby around the middle.

Sometimes, I turned to the side to see how ugly my overbite looked with my braces. And other times, when I washed my hands, I stared at them because I couldn't face myself in the mirror.

Did I include too much about the mirror? I thought sometimes that redundancy had meaning.

My friends liked to tease me because they loved how mad it made me. One time, I told them to stop while we were in Spanish class, and they asked me why. I burst out, "It hurts!" and with no exaggeration, the entire class grew silent.

Or maybe that is an exaggeration. I was also prone to exaggeration.

The night my grandfather called to tell us he had cancer was the first time I'd ever seen my mother cry when she wasn't watching a movie. I held it together for her sake, pulling out a chair for her, and hugging her, but when I went upstairs, I sobbed in my shower.

Cliché.

I stared at my razor, feeling a strange urge, but I turned off the shower and dried off instead.

The next day was the talent show at school. I was playing the piano and my friend was singing, and I was nervous and messed up badly. I left the room crying. The principal ran after me and I told her that my grandfather had cancer. I still don't know if that was the reason I cried, or if I was just embarrassed about messing up. She invited me to come back inside, and I dug my nails deep into my arm. I didn't know what I was doing.

After another beating session of sleep away camp, eighth grade made me want to stop waking up in the morning.

Melodramatic.

I felt waves of heavy pain in my chest that left me crying by myself in my room, or I felt nothing at all. I began to crave pain, so I joined ~~Cross Country~~ cross country, hoping that exercise would be enough. I smiled because I read that smiling makes you feel happier. I double pierced my ears as a reminder to stop thinking dark thoughts, but they didn't go away.

If I keep writing this, people are going to think I'm looking for attention.

Culture Shock

At the beginning of eighth grade, my best friend and I began Skyping each other on a regular basis. We made a promise that if anybody said anything about one of us, we would tell each other. I told her that when people talked behind her back, they thought she was perfect and they loved her.

She told me that my other best friend hated me. In a rant about me, she said I was annoying, a follower. I bragged too much about running. I was terrible at art and I wasn't going to get into the magnet art high school I was applying to.

I left the computer a few times to grab tissues, in convulsive tears. When I logged off, I couldn't stop shaking. I saved the chat into my phone, and labeled it as "Reminder." I wrote down a quote, "I'm not going to stop running, I won't stop drawing, and I won't stop being who I am, whether she likes it or not. I want to write my life. I hold the pen, not her." I went into the shower and stared at my razor again. I picked it up and set it back down.

Way too melodramatic.

I didn't tell anybody about it. I bought a notebook and wrote a plan to get my friend to stop hating me:

- "She said I was too modest. Be proud of yourself."
- "Do not say anything about your appearance that you don't like. Rather, compliment others"
- "If you are teased, don't deny it, just say I guess you are right, thanks for telling me"

- "Do not act angry whenever something she does aggravates you"
- "Step away if she wants to be with the popular people
- "Always be in a happy, agreeable mood unless something bad happens."
- "Do not keep your hands clasped together. It makes you look pathetic."

I've never actually confronted my friend, and we're still friends today. We've both changed, and I've forgiven her.

Too apologetic. I'm just guilty for writing about her doing something that isn't relevant anymore.

The night before Yom Kippur, at Kol Nidrei services, I was wearing flats with sharp jewels on them. There was a mosquito bite on my leg, so I scratched it with my foot. The jewel was sharp against my skin and it hurt. I dug the jewel as hard as I could into my leg and pulled down to my ankle. I looked down and saw drops of blood sliding down my leg. I tapped my mom's shoulder and pointed to the cut and whispered, "I started randomly bleeding." She gave me a tissue to stop the bleeding, and I went to the bathroom to wash my cut. I knew I had done it on purpose.

The Internet said that depression was a lasting feeling of sadness for over two weeks. I couldn't remember the last time I was happy. I wrote in my journal that I was "living in Hell. Never has life seemed so dark and endless… I feel guilty for worrying about myself and being depressed when I have everything."

Like any responsible middle schooler, I decided to tell my parents. They didn't believe me. I told them I had cut myself on purpose. Then they were worried. They took me to the doctor, who felt around my thyroid for enlargement. She made me promise not to hurt myself again, and I said okay.

My grandfather died shortly after my first therapy session, and I barely felt anything. I did not dye my hair a different color or wear dark makeup. I wore one set of black earrings and one set of white. At school, I wandered the halls during lunch. I left every class to use the bathroom, where I stood in front of the mirror for five minutes, ashamed to look at myself.

Is this still too much with the mirror?

I imagined I was living in a pit, falling into darkness with walls too slick to climb out. The principal called my mom because she was concerned about me. My mom came into the school and told her and the guidance counselor that I had started therapy. I was so embarrassed. I told my siblings I was going to a doctor for my bad foot. I wrote melodramatic poems about walking on broken glass on little scraps of paper, with desperate and trite lines like, "Fine, you don't see me, but at least hear me out!" and "A soul is left unheard." Before I went to sleep, I calculated my status in the pit. I was at the bottom, clawing at the wall.

I've only broken one promise in my life.

Really? That seems unrealistic.

Eventually, I couldn't resist anymore. When I was in class, I slid a bent paperclip or a sharp ring inside my sweater. At home, it was my compass or scissors or even combs, which actually stung a lot more than you might think. I took plastic forks from the cafeteria and kept them in my pocket because the school didn't have knives. I had to wear my jacket all the time, even during gym class, when I was sweating.

Besides the first time I ever hurt myself, I never bled again. I wanted to. I used to dig my nails into my skin and hope that I could draw blood. But I never got out a knife. I was scared of cutting a vein and dying, which I guess was a good sign, but not bleeding made me feel like I was a fraud.

I was a fraud.

My parents tried to help, they really did. I came down the stairs, looking like always did in those days, dark circles under my eyes, a prominent frown, and my dad said, "Come on, snap out of it." But I couldn't.

Too abstract. What do I mean I couldn't?

I just couldn't.

I wrote journal entries about wanting to end it all: "The weekend was awful. I 'cut,' almost threw up on purpose, obsessed about food, and wanted to die." My therapist told me to write down three things I was thankful for every day. On a bad day I wrote:
1. I got my camp yearbook today
2. I didn't kill myself
3. I didn't find an object sharp enough to bleed when I cut.

Culture Shock

Once on vacation I looked over the balcony on our top story hotel room. *Just jump*, I thought, *I could just jump right now*. But I stayed away from the ledge. We took hikes, surrounded ~~my~~ by cliffs. *Imagine jumping*, I thought, *you could jump*. But I stayed on the path. Standing on edges and holding sharp knives gave me a surge of power that made me afraid.

I told two of my friends.

Liar! I wrote that I didn't have friends earlier.

I thought I scared them off. One of them wrote stories about being depressed. I was annoyed with her because I was sure that I could be the only person who had ever been depressed. I was sick of routine, of everything. Feeling tired the day of the pre-audition workshop for the magnet art school, I decided I didn't want to apply. My mom forced me into the building. So I threw myself into writing to prepare for the audition. That helped, I think.

One night I wrote the things I was thankful for at the bottom of my journal:

1. A girl said I have a kind heart
2. I felt happy for a portion of today
3. My pieces are perfect for my piano test.

In March, I began to climb out of the pit, sometimes slipping, but actually aiming for the top this time. I was in my school play, where I was surrounded by laughter. It's a bit hard to be depressed when people are counting on you to pretend to be happy. You start to believe it. I got into the magnet school. I could look in the mirror and see that my stomach was mostly flat, and despite the bad flare-up of acne, I could look pretty sometimes. I started running for the joy of it, not for the pain. I began to thaw.

Is that really the right word? A chicken thaws on the counter. People don't.

One night, the pain of my grandfather's death hit me and I cried for him.

A few months later, I opened a drawer in the bathroom out of curiosity and found an envelope from my therapist. Inside was my diagnosis: an adjustment disorder with mixed anxiety and depressed mood. I put the paper back in the envelope and slid it into the drawer. It took a few years for it to start making sense.

And here we are, the present. This March, I've gone five years without "cutting." As much as I pretend those horrible years ~~has~~ have nothing to do with my life now, I know they do. I always assume people will dislike me when they meet me.

Do you dislike me?

I tend to put myself down. I catch myself hearing that girl from camp, *Why are you always following us? It makes you look pathetic.*

I'm trying to get rid of her. That nagging voice, that perfect girl. But she's still there, buried underneath. She comes out through panic attacks, exercising six days a week, practicing the piano every night, straight As. She fights the urge to delete the last sentence because she knows it makes me look perfect.

Culture Shock

I'm trying to understand her ~~to~~ too. I can't shake the feeling that I will fight her for the rest of my life.

I recently made the decision not to get braces for the third time, even though my teeth are still slightly crooked. I'm not quite sure why I wrote that, but it seems to mean something.

Long Lost

When I was in seventh grade, my Jewish History class was assigned a family history project. We were instructed to create tri-fold boards with essays on our family history, pictures, timelines, and family crests based on the meaning of our last names. With the librarian's help, I found a book that tracked "Rubenchick" back to Biblical times. It was supposedly derived from the tribe of Rueben.[1] In the Diaspora, the history of Rueben became lost, as Jews dispersed and spread to different corners of the globe. It was possible that a few members of the tribe ended up in a small shtetl on the outskirts of Minsk, but I knew nothing of my family history beyond my great grandfather. Eventually, I created my family crest with a mandrake, which my teacher told me was a symbol for the tribe of Reuben.

For the project, I interviewed my zayde about my great grandfather. I learned how he escaped, with Russian and Polish soldiers shooting at him from both

---

[1] One of the twelve tribes of Israel, descendant from Jacob's eldest son, Reuben

Culture Shock

sides, and how he was almost sent back to Russia after traveling on a crowded ship to America. However, what struck me the most about his story was the family still in Russia.

My friend and I worked on the project together at her house. When my mother came to pick me up, I was finishing up the story.

"So we have long lost relatives in Russia," I concluded.

"You know, Manny found them, right?" my mom said.

I sought out my great uncle Manny at a Bar Mitzvah party a few weeks later, and finally, the whole story came together.

While they were still in Poland, Sophie's mother discovered from a friend that Yaacov had another family in Russia. She confronted him in a restaurant, and he admitted it. Sophie found out from her mother and went to the river to throw herself in. Yaacov came and stopped her, and they made peace. Considering that they had no money for food or to support their family, and they counted themselves lucky to survive to the next day, another marriage was not a big deal.

My great grandfather's other family was still struggling on the other side of the world. In 1930, Yaacov's father Mordechai died of a heart attack. The same year, Sophie gave birth to a son, whom they named Mordechai. Shortly after Moe's birth, Yaacov returned to Uzlian and stayed for several months.

Yaacov's oldest daughter, Yentl, who later became known as Yelena, like Helen, married a Jewish man by the name of Goldberg. He became a high-ranking officer in the Russian navy on the Black Sea, which was unheard of for a Jew. They lived in Sevastopol, Crimea, with their two sons. The younger daughter was named Shulamit. She married a non-Jewish Russian man, Leonid Podnosov, called Lonya, and they had a son, Igor.

In June, 1941, the Germans invaded the Soviet Union. Whenever and wherever Jews were found, they were killed. Lonya hid Shulamit. He obtained the internal passport of a Russian woman, who was Shulamit's age and had recently died. This woman was named Tamara, so Shulamit took the name Tamara.

When my parents named my sister Tamara, they were unaware that this was not my zayde's sister's given name. Strangely, my mother's Hebrew name is Shulamit. Maybe by the power of coincidence, I am connected to my "long lost" family through unexpected ties. One night at Shabbat dinner, Zayde recalled his father's unusual, thin, and angular fingers. Shulamit's were the same. My sister and I held up our hands, and my grandparents exclaimed that our fingers were similarly shaped to my great grandfather's.

Tamara's new identity was enough to save her from death, but as a Russian woman, she was taken to a slave labor camp in Germany, where she worked until she was transferred to a farm in Northern France.

Culture Shock

There, the labor was completed entirely by Russian women, closely guarded by the Gestapo. They picked potatoes or did other farm work to provide food for the German army. After the war, Tamara was liberated by the Americans and had a choice: to start a new life or "go back to that hellhole"[2] of the Soviet Union. Although her mother and uncles and aunts died in the Minsk ghetto, she had a husband and a son who both survived. She had to go back. Once she arrived, the KGB put her under observation because anyone who could have survived was thought to be a collaborator with the Germans. Under observation for many years, she nevertheless succeeded in becoming a high school teacher of Russian literature. She and her husband had another son, Yevgeny, called Genya, in 1950. She was an intellectual, like her father, but unlike him, Tamara had had enough of being Jewish. Under the Germans, being Jewish was a death sentence, and under the communists, it was a persecution and an unemployment sentence. She didn't raise her boys Jewish, which disappointed her father. This seemed unfair, considering what her Judaism had put her through, but Manny said that his father was "not known for being a fair person."

The Cold War began in the late 1940s, while Jews were coping with the horrific aftermath of the Holocaust. During this time, American distaste for Communism

---

[2] In the words of my great uncle Manny

turned to fear and then to intense hatred. America also hated Joseph Stalin, who was responsible for the deaths of forty million people during his rule. Meanwhile, the Soviet Union resented the States for entering the war late enough for the Soviet Union to lose eleven million soldiers and between seven million to twenty million civilians. Tensions rose as the Soviet Union intended to expand into Eastern Europe and felt threatened by U.S. interventionism and accumulation of arms. With the loss of almost forty percent of the world's Jews, life was uncertain for Jews at best.

Anti-Semitism in Russia did not improve. In 1954, Stalin accused nine doctors, six of them Jewish, of trying to poison leaders in the Soviet Union. The men were arrested and tortured until Stalin died before the trial began. Eventually, the Soviet Union adopted a policy forbidding Jews to leave. Still, a number of Jews, who became known as refuseniks, applied for exit visas. In return, they were fired from their jobs. Other work was impossible to find because the communist government was the sole Russian employer. Government restrictions forbade Jews from practicing Judaism and engaging in religious life.

In 1959, nearing the height of the Cold War, Yaacov Rubin returned to Minsk to visit what remained of his family. A year later, Manny made the journey to find his sisters. He met Tamara and quickly bonded with her over Yiddish, their common

Culture Shock

language.[3] Although Tamara resented her father for deserting her family, she didn't blame Manny. He and Tamara corresponded frequently, although their letters often took months to arrive. It was possible that the KGB had inspected the letters, but they were written in Yiddish, which was practically a secret code. Neither Manny nor his father could visit Yelena because if the Soviet Union found out that her husband had American relatives, that would end his career.

About every two years, Manny visited Tamara and her husband. He stayed in a hotel, but Tamara's family prepared banquets for him. In their eyes, he was "a visitor from Mars, a space alien." The youngest son, Genya didn't believe a word he said and asked millions of questions. Before Manny's first visit, they had never met an American before.

Yelena's husband retired from the Soviet navy, and they returned to Minsk. Manny tried to reach out to them, but she refused to meet him. She feared the effect on her husband's pension and status, and she resented her father, a sentiment that extended to Manny. Finally, on one of Manny's visits to Tamara, Yelena expressed desire to meet the "space alien." She

---

[3] Manny was different from his brothers in that he spoke only Yiddish until he was five or six years old. When his family struggled in the Great Depression, Manny had been sent to live with his maternal grandparents in Brooklyn. They didn't speak English, so Manny spoke with them in Yiddish. His father taught him Judaic studies at home, so Manny didn't attend public school until second grade.

and Manny met on a park bench in one of Minsk's central parks. Manny only knew a few dirty words in Russian, and Yelena didn't even know dirty words in English, so they spoke Yiddish. Manny met Yelena's younger son Eugene, who hated the Soviets.

"I will never be able to get out of here," he told Manny. Eventually he did, after the collapse of the Soviet Union in 1991. But until then, he could only look forward to Manny's visits to their apartment.

Manny's younger brother Yussel also visited his sisters. He brought yarmulkes and prayer books, which were illegal. As he was walking down the street at night, a man pulled him into an alley and asked if he was a Jew. It was risky, but Yussel admitted he was. The man beckoned him to an apartment, which was filled with other Jewish Russians, wanting to meet an American Jew. Together, they listened to jazz, talked about their lives and what it meant to be a Jew.

In the 1970s, the Soviet Union refused to give Manny a visa to visit. He was not able to return until the winter of 1991, when he represented the American government to establish a new institute. His wife bought him a large white feather down coat. He went to Moscow and visited his family in Minsk. Shortly after, the Soviet Union collapsed.

After the dissolution, Manny had trouble bringing Tamara over to America. Because her internal passport was Russian, she was not recognized as Jewish. At this point, Lonya had died, and she remarried a Jewish man who had children in Denver.

Culture Shock

She brought her younger son Genya. Igor followed a few years later. Today, Tamara's sons live in Denver with their families. Genya has a daughter named Tanya, who has grown close to my father after meeting each other at Manny's son's Bar Mitzvah.

On Yelena's side of the family, Eugene came to America first, married for a second time to a woman named Marina, who was already in the States under a refugee program. He got a job as a clean room technician in a facility that manufactured electronic chips for antimissile programs. Marina learned English well and worked in a nonprofit organization for various charities in Connecticut. They had a son named Alexei. Yelena's older son, Gregory was a professor of mathematics and had a job at a bank during the recession, until that branch was closed down. His son, Povell, who is my father's age, lives in San Francisco and works as a financial analyst.

When my father was growing up, he didn't know that his mother had a sister. He found out when he was in college, or maybe even older. My great aunt Mona married a non-Jew and lost touch with the family. My father found out that he had two cousins, who were policemen in New York. The older son, Teddy, moved to Hong Kong, and my father met Kenny for the first time at my parents' wedding. My parents were living in New Jersey met occasionally with Kenny in New York. Once my father and Kenny realized they shared a love for poker, they become closer friends. He introduced Kenny to my siblings and me, and two years ago, we attended his wedding.

Other relatives have resurfaced in recent years. I once found a photograph of a little girl in a family album and asked my father who she was. It was his cousin Shaina, and they hadn't spoken in years. When my father was out of college, he babysat for his uncle Asher's two toddlers, Jacob and Shaina, in San Francisco. As the children grew older, they lost touch. A few years ago, when she was an adult out of law school, Shaina reached out to us and asked to come over to Passover. We invited her and her boyfriend and attended their wedding two years later.

One of Yaacov's brothers had a son who survived the Holocaust. His name was Yoseph Rubenchick.[4] He was married to a woman named Mana, who was a physician. She died in Minsk from a stroke. After the collapse of the Soviet Union, Yoseph made his way to Israel and reunited with his sons and daughter.

Inspired by Manny and my father, I logged onto Facebook and typed "Rubenchick." All the results were Israeli women. One of them was wearing a blue lace cardigan. Another was her mother, with a round face and dyed black hair. I couldn't know if we were related; still, I scrolled through and saw that she had two sons, and one of them recently had a birthday.

---

[4] Like my great uncle Yussel, or Yoseph. However, just like my sister Tamara, their parents had no knowledge of this when naming their children.

Culture Shock

Another Rubenchick woman, perhaps her cousin, had a young daughter and son. They were pictured on a boat, the boy climbing on the deck in his swim trunks. The girl posed in a pink dress on a cobblestone walk with a brown picket fence. Their friends had Hebrew names and Russian names. I can only wonder.

SJH: Alexander the Great to Non-Muslim Restrictions

- In 334 BCE, Alexander the Great defeats the Persians and allows the Jews to remain under a theocracy. In Jewish history, Alexander's one of the good guys.
- Following the death of Alexander, King Antiochus takes over and forbids the practice of Judaism. He and his men desecrate the temple. Led by Judah the Maccabee and the rest of the Hasmonaean family, the Jews revolt. They win the fight, enter Jerusalem, and purify the temple. Legend has it that there was only enough oil in the temple to light the Menorah for a day; still, it lasted for eight. Today, Hanukkah is an excuse to eat fried donuts and potato pancakes, honoring the old Jewish saying: "They tried to kill us. They failed. Let's eat."
- In 63 CE, Roman general Pompey captures Jerusalem. Under Roman rule, twelve disciples believe that their savior, the messiah, could be a Jewish teacher known as Jesus of Nazareth. Not big fans of any unruliness, the Romans nail Jesus to a cross and kill him.

Culture Shock

- According to Jewish law, the messiah has to be alive, but with believed sightings of Jesus back from the dead, an argument begins in the Jewish community. Those who believe Jesus to be the messiah branch off into a sect of Judaism that becomes Christianity. Those who do not believe are left waiting for the messiah to this day.
- In the year 66 BCE, the Jews revolt against the Romans. In return, the Romans destroy Jerusalem and the second Temple in 70 BCE. The temple is never rebuilt, and Jewish leaders are exiled, killed, or taken as slaves.
- From 132-135, the remaining Jews fight against the Romans in the Bar Kokba revolt. They are ultimately defeated in the battle of Bethar.
- In the 300s, the Byzantines conquer the land. Emperor Constantine adopts Christianity, and Israel becomes predominantly Christian. The Jews lose their right to hold public positions and are forbidden from entering Jerusalem except on *Tisha B'Av,* the anniversary of the destruction of the second temple, to mourn.
- In 614, the Jews aid the Persian invasion, in hopes of deliverance by the messiah. The messiah never arrives, but Persia grants the Jews administration of Jerusalem.
- A little over ten years later, the Byzantine army regains the city, and expels the Jews.

- The prophet Muhammad dies in 632, and the Islamic Empire reigns for more than four centuries. Jews are granted permission to live under "protection," the status of non-Muslims under Islamic rule. In exchange for poll and land taxes, Jews are given the right to own property, engage in commerce, and practice their religion, just as long as they don't practice publicly or convert anyone.
- In 691, Caliph Abd el-Malik marks Jerusalem as a holy site by building the Dome of the Rock on the site of the First and Second Temples. It's a time of peaceful coexistence and exchange of cultural values, "The Golden Age," if you will.
- In 717, restrictions are placed on non-Muslims. Jews have to wear a special yellow garment for the first time and certainly not the last time. There are heavy taxes on agricultural land. Jews have to move from rural areas to towns, where they are faced with social and economic discrimination. Many are forced to leave the country. By the end of the eleventh century, there are hardly any Jews left in the land, and they lose track of each other. Judaism is not organized as it once was.

Jew-ish

Our first home in Baltimore bordered a secluded, almost exclusively Jewish cul-de-sac. Still, my family was the only one who kept kosher and said prayers over Shabbat meals every Friday. Once, after returning from Yom Kippur services at synagogue, I visited my neighbor, who had been playing videogames all morning. He told me that he thought my family was ultra-religious.

I told him that was absurd. "We just drove on Yom Kippur,"[1] I said. He didn't understand why that mattered. I repeated that I was not religious and wondered why being more Jewish than my neighbor made me defensive.

I experienced similar discomfort when my grandparents lived in Nashville, and we attended services at their Orthodox synagogue for Rosh Hashanah, the Jewish New Year. The men sat in the center of the congregation, while the women sat on elevated platforms behind walls on either side, so we could watch over the service, but the men had to look

---

[1] You're not supposed to drive on Yom Kippur

up to see us. If that wasn't enough separation, there was a balcony in the back of the synagogue, where women could sit behind a fence. When I was much tinier, I stood on my tiptoes to see the rabbi blow the *shofar*.[2] He was a professional trumpet player, so the sound was loud and clear, but I longed to stand beside my father, who was only a few feet from the rabbi.

Of the three main sects of Judaism, Orthodox is the most traditional, the one that most closely resembles the shtetl lives of our past, a time when men wore dark coats with *tzizit*[3] underneath, round fur hats atop their *payot*.[4] Their wives covered their hair, had many children, and were responsible for the cooking and caring of the children. Today, these families congregate in Jerusalem, New York, and many parts of Baltimore. They pray *shacharit*[5] every morning, the men on one side of the *mehitzah*[6], with the women on the other. They believe the Torah was given to Moses by God and is the authority of Judaism. Today, Orthodox Judaism has broken into sects. On one end

---

[2] A hollow ram's horn used as a musical instrument for religious purposes

[3] Knotted tassels on the bottom of a tallit or worn on pants, as a reminder of religious obligation

[4] Side curls worn by men and boys

[5] Morning prayers. There also Mincha, afternoon prayer, and Maariv, evening prayer. Some prayers are repeated more than once.

[6] The wall separating men and women. In some synagogues, this has been a glass, see-through divide, with equally sized men and women sections. In other synagogues, it feels more like a cage.

Culture Shock

of the spectrum are Haredi Jews, who believe that modernism is a distraction and incompatible with Jewish tradition. On the other, Modern Orthodox Jews believe it is possible to remain observant and engage with the modern, secular world.

During the French Revolution, a large number of Jews converted to Christianity or pulled away from Jewish communities, schools, and universities. Reform Judaism began when Jewish academic Leopold Zunz proposed an alternative solution: Jews should study Jewish history and Torah, while incorporating local music and language. Shortly after, Rabbi Abraham Geiger observed that change had always been necessary in Jewish life to make it easier to practice, and therefore, appeal to modern people. When European Jews immigrated to the United States in the 1830s, Reform Judaism became the dominant form of Judaism. Today, many American Jews are Reform. They're what my father calls "Jewish in name only." Many do not keep kosher, do not attend Jewish day school, and do not fast on Yom Kippur.

I'm a Conservative Jew. Conservatives understood that it was difficult, if not impossible, to maintain an ancient code of law in a rapidly changing world, but according to the teachings of Zacharias Frankel and Solomon Schechter, we thought the Reform movement was abandoning too much of Judaism. So we met in the middle, turning to modernism more slowly and more cautiously than Reform Judaism. For example, in 1883, word spread of non-Kosher food served at the celebration of the first graduates of the Hebrew Union College, a Reform institute for training rabbis. After this event, the Conservative movement was officially established.

Jewish traditions differ based on sect, family, and origin: Ashkenazi, who originate from Europe, and Sephardi, who originate from the Middle East. Some holidays in Ashkenazi tradition are a day longer than in Sephardi tradition. When the prophets lived in Israel, the beginning of the month and the beginning of holidays were dependent on eye-witnesses to the new moon, who testified before the Rabbinic Court that they had seen the moon. However, due to slow communication, the rabbis worried that distant communities might not hear about the holiday in time. To prevent people from missing the holy first day, cities in the Diaspora were given an extra day. Even with modern technological and communication advances, Ashkenazi holidays still follow this tradition.

When I consider what they must look like to the outsider, Jewish traditions are strange. Take for example, the process of fulfilling the covenant. Brit Milah, or circumcision, occurs on the eighth day after a baby boy is born. The mother carries her infant to the front of the room and places him in the arms of a designated female, who gives him to a designated male, who brings him to the circumcision table. A chair is designated for the prophet Eliyahu. Someone is given the honor of placing the baby on the chair, as the *mohel*, or the ritual circumciser, chants and asks

Culture Shock

Eliyahu for nothing to go wrong during the circumcision. Then someone else lifts the baby and gives him to the father, who places the baby in the lap of the sandek, the person who holds the baby down during the circumcision. With six male grandchildren, my zayde was given this job every time. There are pictures of him, turning from the baby with a look of disdain. In February, when my last of twelve cousins was born, he handed the honor off to my uncle. When the baby is secured, the father hands the surgical knife to the mohel, who recites a blessing and begins circumcision. A second sandek holds the infant as the mohel recites the blessings, and finally, the name of the baby is revealed. Everyone drinks wine, and the mohel dips his pinky into the wine to feed a few drops to the baby to ease the pain. Then, as always in Jewish traditions, everyone joins in a festive meal of bagels, lox, and egg salad.

Even as a Jew, traditions are confusing, so I will try to cover the basics of a Jewish year:

The fall is jam-packed with Jewish holidays. We bring in the New Year with Rosh Hashanah, one of the big three holidays mentioned in the Bible, along with Yom Kippur and Passover. Rosh Hashanah is one of those holidays whose duration depends on location. In Israel, Rosh Hashanah is one day. In Diaspora communities, it's two.

On Rosh Hashanah, we have a seder, or ritual dinner, where it is customary to eat the heads of fish, to represent the beginning of things. Challot are baked in a circle to represent the cycle of life. We eat apples and honey for a sweet new year. At synagogue, the rabbi blows the shofar as the cantor calls out different rhythms. As fun as this holiday may be, it's called the Day of Judgment, when God inscribes you in the book of life to live or die in the next year. We repent for our misdeeds of the past year and recite the *Tashlikh* prayer, throwing bread into rivers to represent the casting away of our sins.

A week later, on Yom Kippur, our fate is sealed in the book of life. The night before, in a ritual called *Kapparot*, it is customary to swing a chicken around your head to atone. Then the chicken is given to the homeless or poor. In Krieger Schechter, we used a rubber chicken. On Yom Kippur, we don't eat, we don't drink, we don't wear luxurious objects. Everyone in synagogue wears his or her nicest white clothing and tennis shoes. You're supposed to abstain from washing or brushing your teeth. Because Judaism follows the lunar calendar, Yom Kippur begins at nightfall. This is the only time men wear their tallitot in the evening. The next day, we spend all morning singing about who shall die and who shall be born, and how the people who shall die, die:

> Who by fire and who by water
> Who by the sword and who by wild beasts
> Who by hunger and who by thirst
> Who by earthquake and who by plague

Culture Shock

> Who by strangling and who by
> stoning. (Unesanneh Tokef Prayer).

Services run until noon, but there are discussions and learning sessions to distract you until evening services. My family always says we'll come back for the evening services, but we're all so miserable that we never make it. I watch Netflix until I never want to see a television screen again and feel guilty when I don't feel like I suffered enough.

The next holiday is Sukkot, where we build giant huts with braches and pine needles on top, called S'chach.[7] We are supposed to eat, sleep, and enjoy each other's company in the sukkahs to commemorate the years the Jews slept in tents in the desert. In synagogue, we hold a *lulav*, a combination of different branches, and an *etrog*, or a citron, and march around the synagogue in a line, shaking it up and down and side to side. I often turn to my father and say, "If someone looked through the window right now, they'd think we were in a cult."

Sukkot ends with Shemini Atzeret, a major holiday where we are prohibited from doing work. On this day, we stop shaking the lulav and the etrog, and although we still eat in the sukkah, we stop reciting blessings about dwelling in it. In synagogue, we recite Yizkor, the memorial prayer. To our daily service, we also add a prayer for rain, which we will recite until Passover, when the rainy season ends in Israel.

---

[7] The most disgusting word in the Hebrew language

The next day is Simchat Torah, one of the most joyful holidays. We complete the Torah and begin it again at Genesis. Then we all grab the Torahs and dance with them in a circle to *Hava Nagila*, a celebrative folk song that is also danced to at Bar Mitzvahs. Our synagogue puts out coolers of ice cream and hands out whole chocolate bars.

After Simchat Torah, there's a slight lull until December, when Hanukkah is usually celebrated. I say usually because the Jewish calendar does not always align with the rest of the world's. A few years ago, we lit Hanukkah candles the night of Thanksgiving.

For seven or eight days (depending on location), we light a menorah[8], adding a candle every night until the entire lamp is lit. At Krieger Shechter, teachers halted lessons for a week to light the *hanukiah*, play with the *dreidel*,[9] and eat jelly donuts. We celebrated the miracle of light because after the dictator Antiochus desecrated the temple, the Maccabees were able to light the Menorah for eight days and eight nights with only a drop of oil left in the canister. As we grew older, we learned that the real

---

[8] Technically, the Menorah was the seven-branched lamp that high priests used to light in the temple. A Hanukkah lamp is called a hanukiah.

[9] A spinning top inscribed with the Hebrew letters "nun," "gimel," "hei," and "shin," which represent the phrase, "a great miracle happened there." In Israel, dreidels are inscribed with a "peh" instead of a "shin," to say "a great miracle happened here."

Culture Shock

miracle of Hanukkah was the Maccabees' ability to defeat the Greek army.

In Israel, when we had the entire week of Hanukkah off school, people swarmed bakeries to buy *sufganiyot*.[10] Unlike the pareve powdered donuts from Seven Mile Market, the local Jewish grocery store in Baltimore, Israel carried fresh fried donuts with gourmet flavors like dulce de leche and double chocolate. From the street, in the back of the line for the bakery, my siblings and I watched an older man shove his way to the front with his enormous belly. In the Schuster Center, a giant *hanukiah* glowed brighter with another candle every night.

A few months later, as the trees begin to thaw and rejuvenate, we celebrate Tu B'shevat, the new year for the trees. As a kid, I went vegetarian in third grade, spent all of my time outdoors, and earned the nickname "nature girl." I had named all of the trees in our yard and was not ashamed to hug them. Tu B'shevat was my favorite holiday. Before the freak Baltimore blizzards or 70 degree temperatures in February, Tu B'shevat was usually a pleasant day in late winter or early February. Sometimes the temperature would be in the 60s, and my siblings and I wore shorts and t-shirts. We held a ceremony in the yard and brought presents for the trees. I took a rock

---

[10] Jelly donuts

from the pile underneath our deck and lay it on the soil of the tree[11] outside my bedroom.

Based on tradition, Tu B'shevat was the day when fruit was counted for tithing. People were prohibited from eating the first three years of their fruit harvest. On the fourth year, they brought the fruit to the temple to be sacrificed. Now, we eat fruits and nuts at a seder in synagogue. People try to avoid eating meat or dairy, which I enjoyed as a vegetarian and enjoy even more as a vegan.

While Purim is arguably a more exciting holiday for a child than Tu B'shevat, I was always conflicted by it. Although we dressed up, exchanged gift baskets, and were encouraged to make as much noise as possible in synagogue, the holiday also fell on my birthday almost every other year. One year I brought donuts to class for my birthday and one of my peers asked if they were from the PTA for Purim.

In synagogue, we read Megillat Esther, which tells another story that fits snugly into the Jewish saying, "They tried to kill us, they failed, let's eat!" The Persian king Achashverosh was advised to replace his queen Vashti after she refused to display herself at one of his six-month celebrations. After a pageant is held for all eligible maidens, Achashverosh chooses a beautiful woman named Esther, without knowing that she is Jewish. He also appoints an anti-Semite named

---

[11] This one was named Sunshine. There was also Mitch, Friend, Shadow, Cyclone, and many more that have already slipped my mind.

Culture Shock

Haman to be the prime minister. When Esther's uncle Mordechai refuses to bow to Haman, Haman becomes so angry that he vows to kill all the Jews. Mordechai seeks Esther's help. Esther decides to throws two banquets for the King and Haman, and in the second one, finally reveals that she is a Jew and that Haman is trying to kill her people. On the day when all the Jews were supposed to be killed, Haman and his sons are hanged instead.

Whenever Haman's name is chanted during the reading, we make obnoxious loud noises with groggers or hand clappers. Eventually, the synagogue made a "start" and "stop" sign because the young children would not stop booing. After the reading is completed, the synagogue throws a party similar to the one during Simchat Torah, with a teen club and a karaoke bar for the parents. If you're legally allowed to, you're supposed to drink until you can't tell the difference between Haman and Mordechai.

Finally, we reach one of the most important Jewish holidays: Passover. Leavened bread, and grains such as wheat, barley, rye, spelt, and oats are prohibited, which means eight days of feeling hungry, especially as a vegetarian and a picky eater. In the Ashkenazi tradition, we are also prohibited from consuming *kidniyot*: legumes, corn, rice, and soy. The rabbis feared that after the harvest, bags of wheat would spill into the bags of kidniyot, so it was better to avoid eating them than risk breaking Passover law. Recently, Ashkenazi rabbis in the Conservative movement changed this law to allow the consumption of kidniyot; however, some traditionalists still refrain from consuming them.

Passover was my favorite holiday because my aunts, uncles, and cousins all traveled to my grandparents' house in Nashville. I would not see them again until Rosh Hashanah. My grandparents invited their other friends, and the room was full, and the seder seemed to last the entire night. A few times, we met at a log cabin in Gatlinburg, where we spent our days looking for crawfish in the creek, playing air hockey, and wrestling in the fields. Eventually, there were ten grandchildren, running around the house in the Passover shirts my bubbe made every year.

seder means order, so the first think you do in a seder is sing about the order:

- Kadesh- we sing Kiddush, or the blessing over the wine, and drink the first cup of wine.
- Urchatz- two designated grandchildren come around with a pitcher and basin so we can wash our hands.
- Karpas- we dip vegetables in salt water.
- Yachatz- we break the middle matzah in a stack of three. The bigger half becomes the *afikoman*,[12] which is wrapped in cloth and left to my uncle

---

[12] Eaten as "dessert" at the end of the meal

for safekeeping. The kids steal the afikoman and hide it.
- Maggid- we recite out of the Haggadah, or the Passover prayer book. It is customary for the youngest child to sing Ma'Nishtanah, or "why is this night different from all other nights?" but in my family, every kid sang it from youngest to oldest until we reached Bar Mitzvah age. After reading the Exodus story, we drink the second cup.
- Rachtzah- we wash our hands again.
- Motze- we recite the blessing over the food.
- Matzah- we bless and eat the matzah
- Marror- we eat the bitter herbs
- Korech- we eat a Hillel sandwich of matzah, bitter herbs, and charoset[13]
- Shulchan Oruch- we finally get to eat the main meal
- Tzafun- we bargain with the adults for presents in exchange for the afikoman.[14] The afikoman is the last thing we eat.

---

[13] A paste made of apples, nuts, and cinnamon
[14] Once when I was little, I felt bad for stealing, so I returned the afikoman early. Everyone still makes fun of me for it.

- Bayrech- after the meal, we recite the *Birkat HaMazon*, or blessing for the food, and drink the third cup of wine. We fill up another cup of wine for Eliyahu the prophet. The kids open the door singing "Eliyahu ha-navi," and the invisible prophet comes in and starts drinking wine. The adults shake the table so it looks like he's drinking.
- Hallel- we sing *Hallel*, or psalms of praise, and drink the fourth cup of wine
- Nirtzah- Finally, we pray that God accepted our service

Immediately after Passover, we begin the Counting of the Omer, the forty-nine day period leading to Shavuot, when people brought offerings of wheat to the temple. It's considered a mourning period because a plague killed 24,000 students of Rabbi Akiva. Weddings are not scheduled during this period. You're not supposed to listen to music or wear new clothes. Men often don't shave. Lag B'Omer is the thirty-third day of this count. The mourning period is lifted for this day only, so on Lag B'Omer, boys get haircuts and couples have their weddings. Children light bonfires and play with bow and arrows.

This is what it means to be a Jew. I've tried to pull back the curtain slightly, to give you a taste, a sound of benching after every meal, a twirl in the

Culture Shock

circular dances my bubbe instructs at Israeli dancing and my cousins' Bar Mitzvahs. However, to completely cover the fundamentals of Judaism, I would need to write a book, specifically, the Torah, *Nevi'im*, the books of the prophets, *Ketuvim*, or writings, the Mishnah, and the Gemara. These books were written through centuries of discussion, persecution, and momentous historical events. Nine years at Jewish Day School barely covered Jewish tradition. Jewish communities are often described as clique-y because we tend to stay together, connected by the practice of traditions that are only understandable to Jews. It's a huge part of our lives and slips into daily interactions. In Baltimore, we all shop at Seven Mile Market. We live in the same neighborhoods. My father likes to post on Facebook that his kids fill him with *naches*[15] and post a second time that his phone autocorrected naches to nachos.

    I took this "Jewish connection" for granted until I moved from day school to public high school and found myself in the minority. I couldn't talk about Shabbat or keeping kosher, natural parts of Jewish life, without having to explain myself. I became drawn to the Jewish people I met. There is relief in having someone understand everything you're saying. You could mention a Hebrew word in passing or talk about an obscure tradition, and people will nod their heads and add their own thoughts.

---

[15] Pride

Elana Rubin

My sophomore year, I joined HaZamir, an international Jewish high school choir. Every year, chapters from Israel and almost every state in America meet for a gala concert in New York. We're all Jewish, and we sing songs in Hebrew or ones that contain English phrases from the Bible. We schedule our gala concerts around Passover, which never falls on the same date each year. The range of three or four weeks when the concert takes place makes sense to all of us and all the people who attend. It's a freeing experience to be surrounded by people like you. It's been commonly said that Jews are a family.[16]

In Israel, we had our first Sephardi Passover, only seven days with one seder. When my family traveled during Passover in the States, we resorted to eating omelets and roasted vegetables, because there was nothing else kosher for Passover. In Israel, most restaurants become kosher for Passover and served kidniyot, following the Sephardi tradition. Allowed to consume rice and soy, we went out for sushi every other day.

We were invited to the seder of our Israeli family friends, whom we had known in the States. They set up a large tent with folding tables and string lights. Everyone wore jeans.

There weren't many differences between a Nashville and a Tel-Aviv service. We ate falafel and eggplant because we were in Israel, but the youngest

---

[16] Quite literally, Jews are all related to some degree

Culture Shock

child still sang the Ma Nishtana, we broke the middle matzah, and this time, the adults hid the afikoman. At the conclusion of the seder, we sang *L'shanah haba'ah b'Yerushalayim*, "Next year in Jerusalem."

What a shame, I thought. We're so close to Jerusalem.

The same year we moved to Israel, my cousins moved to Barbados. My aunt works for the United States' Centers for Disease Control and Prevention, and she chose the Caribbean to study AIDS. The government put her family up in a large house surrounded by tropical plants and a pool in the back. My three cousins, the Albalaks, were sent to the international school.

The first time we visited my cousins, I was surprised to find a synagogue, especially a crowded one. Combined with Caribbean humidity, the packed room became hot and sweaty. Barbados's capitol, Bridgetown, is home to the oldest synagogue in the entire Western Hemisphere. Jews arrived in Barbados in 1628. It is believed that they brought sugar to the Caribbean. The Jews prospered for a short time, but by the 1920s, few Jews were left in Barbados. Following WWII, the community grew slightly as Jews migrated out of Europe. Currently, the Jewish community consists of maybe fifty people. They have no rabbi. Two members of the congregation take turns leading Shabbat services. On high holidays, like Rosh Hashanah and Yom Kippur, a rabbi comes down from New York. Everyone was happy with this arrangement.

They welcomed newcomers, men and women sat together, and prayers were read in both English and Hebrew.

Then, the Chabad movement sent a family of Orthodox Jews to Barbados. To increase the small amount of Jewish education my cousins could receive in the Caribbean, my aunt and uncle sent them to this family's townhouse for private lessons. My cousins grew suspicious that this family was not actually sent by Chabad. They were quirky and went on tirades about the Messiah, and my family had known most members of Chabad to be tolerant and open-minded.

The Albalaks were invited to the Chabad family's Passover seder. They arrived on time at five that evening and were shuttled through the kitchen, where the tabletops and cabinets were covered completely in tinfoil. The basement was cramped, and the corners were filled with dust and hair. The family had managed to squeeze in a plastic table surrounded by low beach chairs. The only other guest was a large Canadian Bajan who spoke Hebrew.

As the rabbi stood to recite blessings from the Haggadah, his two young daughters ran at my aunt and began to pull her hair and brush it with a plastic comb. Throughout the service, the rabbi's wife prepared food upstairs, shouting down to her husband every few minutes. He was used to ignoring her. She returned in time for Yachatz, the breaking of the middle matzah of the three matzot on the seder plate for the afikoman. The Rabbi held up the matzah, and it broke into two equal parts. Everyone stared for a minute. Despite its perforations, matzah is crumbly and uncooperative. You just can't break a matzah perfectly in half. This struggle is so common that one of the biggest frustrations of Passover is being forced to eat matzah sandwiches on uneven halves. The middle matzah has a special name, *Levi,* in the middle of the *Kohen* and *Yisrael* matzot. They couldn't just choose a different middle matzah to break. This was a disaster. The wife and the Rabbi argued about which half to use for the afikoman, throwing Bible passages at one another. After an intense debate, the left half was used.

Later, it was time to make the Hillel sandwich. Along with bitter herbs and charoset, lettuce was introduced at this seder. However, the lettuce had to be dry. A single drop of water that touched the matzah would turn it into leavened bread. The Rabbi dried every piece of lettuce with toilet paper and examined it against the light, wiping it with his fingers.

"This one's fine," he said. "Please pass it down to Ari." The lettuce was passed through the hands of every person at the table and fell on the floor before it reached Ari. He picked it up, and at that moment, saw a giant cockroach running up the wall and lost his appetite anyway.

Time passed slowly in the basement. When dinner finally arrived, it was a half-cooked chicken, a lettuce and carrot salad, and more matzah. The

Albalaks stared at the food in front of them and commented on how lovely everything was.[17]

The rabbi, who had become drunk on Manishewitz, insisted they stay for dessert. As the wife began to go upstairs to prepare it, my cousin Liyat needed to use the bathroom. The wife tried to open the bathroom door, but it was locked from the inside. The wife began shouting about his drunkenness and inability to maintain a bathroom. My aunt insisted that Liyat could wait. The other guest, who had been silent in the corner, suggested using a credit card to jimmy open the door, and that worked.

Dessert was a combination of banana and mandarin oranges in thick syrup. As the third cup of wine was poured, the children went upstairs to welcome Eliyahu. My cousins considered making a run for it, but returned to the cold basement and sang L'shanah haba'ah b'Yerushalayim, hoping that next year they'd be anywhere but in that basement.

Less than a year later, the Barbadian government evicted the family for lack of documentation. My cousins never saw them again. Ari remarked that their seder, while unusual, still followed the traditional order.

On a family trip to Mexico, I met a group of friends who were also on vacation. One of the girls was Jewish, and we spent the first night talking about being

---

[17] "At that moment in time, being enslaved in Egypt didn't seem all that bad," Ari said.

Culture Shock

Jewish while our other friends played with the food on their plates, unable to follow along. Once, my family took a trip to Croatia with our family friends. We were seated outside, eating in a non-kosher restaurant, and my friend ordered calamari. Still, a group of Hassidic Jews overheard that we were Jewish as they passed our table.

"Do you need a place to stay for Shabbat?" they asked. We thanked them and said we had a place. Really, we would be on a boat cruising the Atlantic Ocean. Suddenly, I felt guilty for not eating a Shabbat dinner, even though my family had never kept Shabbat. I had not expected to find Jews in Croatia. Yet, there they were, walking down the hot cobblestone streets with their tophats, tzizit, and large black jackets, the same picture you'd see in Brooklyn or Jerusalem.

Sunrise, Sunset

Watching *Fiddler on the Roof* is an important rite of passage for young Jewish children. I first saw the play at a community dinner theatre, laughing with Tevye as he shimmied across the barn, terrified, but unable to turn away from Fruma Sarah hollering from stilts, in tears as Tevye turned away from Chaveleh after she eloped with a Christian man named Fyedkah. The first time I saw the movie was on the floor of my Jewish history class at Krieger Schechter Day School when I was in seventh grade.

    The final echo of "Anatevkah," as the fiddler comes off the roof is always moving and always feels important in a way that's difficult to explain. Of course, it's not easy to describe what you feel looking into the lives of what could have easily been your ancestors. Perhaps it's because it doesn't feel like we're seeing our ancestors in *Fiddler on the Roof*. We're seeing ourselves. Much like its opening song, "Tradition" is a staple of Judaism. Every year, we celebrate the same holidays. We keep kosher. We respect our rabbis and expect them to guide us. We take pilgrimages to Israel. Jewish names repeat themselves. Leah, Lila, Naomi,

Culture Shock

Sarah, Rebecca, Isaac, Noah, Jacob, Daniel. In Ashkenazi tradition, we do not name our children after those who are still living, but they serve as a memory of those who died. My middle name, Molly, commemorates the life of my great grandmother. My sister's name, Tamara, comes from our long lost family in Russia, and her middle name, Alexandra, comes from my mother's grandfather, Alexander. My brother's middle name, Charles, is after my father's great uncle who had recently passed away.

The first Jewish wedding I ever saw was in *Fiddler on the Roof.* Illuminated by candles, Motel and Tzeitel pass the Kiddush cup between them. Surrounded by the haunting melody of "Sunrise, Sunset," the community turns inward, watching the ceremony, men and women separated on either side by the chuppah. Then, as the last note fades, Motel crushes the glass cup beneath his foot and the scene erupts into celebration.

My aunt and uncle's wedding began as traditional Jewish weddings do with *Bedeken Di Kallah*, the Veiling of the Bride, a tradition based on the bible story of Jacob and Rachel. Even though he worked seven years to marry Rachel, her father offered Jacob his eldest daughter, Leah. Jacob accidentally married Leah, so now the groom "checks" to make sure he's marrying the right woman. My aunt walked down the aisle to "Sunrise, Sunset," played by a fiddle quartet in my grandparents' synagogue in Nashville where my uncle grew up. She circled my uncle seven times, they blessed the wine and exchanged rings.

One part of this wedding differed from other modern Jewish weddings in that my uncle brought a dowry. Halfway through the ceremony, the fiddles took up a hoedown song as my uncle walked down the aisle and out the door and returned leading four goats. They walked down the aisle, spread feed over the carpet, and the trainer hurried back to remove them. Later, the synagogue put a ban on farm animals after the goats defecated on the new carpet.

For a modern Jewish family living in the suburbs, one important tradition is summer camp. First it was Beth T'filoh, where a bus picked me up from my driveway every morning. We spent the day reapplying sunscreen, swimming, and sucking on popsicles in the shade. Then it was sleep away camp. My first experience was a two week program at Capital Camps, with a spotless dining hall and air conditioned bunks. The first night, there was a thunderstorm, and everyone was crying. I remembered my parents were sailing in the British Virgin Islands and started crying too, while the counselors comforted me and told me the storm wouldn't reach the Caribbean from Rockville. On Shabbat, we wore white and joined in the pavilion to sing the new songs we had learned during our music activity. I made friends too. One girl showed me the book she was reading, *The Hobbit,* which I took out from the library when I returned home. I told another girl about my imaginary pet squirrel named Squa, who I saw jumping over shadows when we drove on the highway. Somehow I managed to keep these friends.

When I came home, I cried the whole day without knowing why. In the end, I decided I didn't want to go back the next year, partially out of embarrassment because everyone knew about my imaginary pet squirrel. I spoke to my camp friend on the phone every night until she sent me a chain email, the kind that says a clown will kill you if you don't send it to ten other people. I was too scared to sleep and my parents wrote my friend not to send me any more chain mail. And that's how our friendship ended.

I wasn't feeling too confident when I joined two of my school friends at another sleep away camp in New Hampshire, Camp Young Judaea. My parents dropped me off at our gate in the airport, where I met my friend. When we arrived in the Manchester airport, no one from the camp was there to receive us. We called the camp, and an hour later, they showed up. We went in for lice checks. The lice ladies went through my hair and thought they found an egg, so they kept me for treatment. When they finished running the lice comb through my hair, there was no sign of any bugs or eggs. They sent me back to meet the rest of my bunk, but not until they had thrown out all of my hair supplies and brush. Luckily, I had a ponytail on my wrist, so I could wrap my oily, treated hair in a bun. The next day, as I was going to my regular activities, the lice ladies called me back for a second treatment. Again, there was nothing in my hair, but "procedure" dictated that they had to treat me. A counselor came to help me wash out my hair. I broke down crying on my bed. Well, actually it was my friend's bed, since mine was a top bunk and I didn't know how to climb up without banging my knee on something. I didn't get a brush for another three days.

I got over it soon enough. I was shy and friends were still hard to come by, but I signed up for electives like arts and crafts and hip-hop. For many clubs, we sat around and talked. The bottom of the bunk became covered in sand, which inevitably ended up in our beds. I spent most of my free time, curled up, reading. I loved it.

My Daled summer, before my sophomore year of high school, the last year of being a regular camper before a trip to Israel the next summer, everything changed. I had come into myself. I made a group of friends who I sat around tables and joked with during free time. I took fitness electives and spent most of my time running. I starred in the camp play as Anna from *Frozen,* joined the voice company, and worked as a waiter.

An hour before it was time to eat, the waiters were called to the dining hall. We took the chairs off the tables, set out plates, cups, and silverware. We put trash bags in metal stands. We had twenty minutes to eat before everyone came in, if we were lucky. Then, we stared at the front where the food would be served from the kitchen, waiting for the counselors to flip the

Culture Shock

number that would call our row. When a row was called, there was a crazed run to the front, where the kitchen staff filled our trays with food, which we would run back to our tables. I always thought I was going to trip, but I never did. This run was easier when I waited the table closest to the window. It was the most difficult when I was all the way in the back of the dining hall. All the food was kosher. When it was a meat meal, there was no diary. When it was a diary meal, there was no meat. I liked dairy meals because I was a vegetarian, and also, because we would likely get ice cream for dessert. After the meal, I took our trash bags outside, tossed them into the dumpster, plugging my nose on the way back to wipe down the tables. I got paid three hundred dollars for the whole summer.

On Shabbat we wore our camp uniforms, had Friday night services, and then went to the dining hall, which was decorated with ceramic plates, real silverware, and rolls of white paper that acted as tablecloths. We served chicken in large metal platters, which I tried to avoid spilling over my white uniform. After the meal and cleanup came the real fun. Counselors stood on chairs to lead traditional camp songs. "The alligator is my friend, he can be your friend to… Tarzan the monkey man… who knows one? I know one!" Then, the music staff got up and played their guitars, and we rose from our tables, found our bunkmates, and danced and sang to Hebrew songs.

Saturday mornings, there were donuts in the dining hall. Following morning services, the rest of the day was free. I found time to run, walk around the camp, and meet at tables in the park to talk with friends. After lunch was another song session: English songs, classic rock, and folksongs, "Build me up Buttercup," "The Middle," "When the Stars Go Blue."

In the third week of the second session, Maccabiah, the camp wide color war, was announced. Our evening activity, "Cool and Creamy," where kids completed challenges while being sprayed with chocolate syrup and whipped cream, was interrupted by a sign, "It's Maccabiah!" It was our Daled year, and twelve of us were chosen as captains. I was not a captain, but all of us got bandanas anyway. I was on the blue team. Most years, I had reluctantly cheered on my teammates and participated in potato sack and three legged races, but this year, I was in charge of the plaque. I designed a concept: America and Israel on either side, a rainbow trailing a ship across the Atlantic Ocean. In the background, I painted the fluffy pink and orange clouds of a sunset.

My chief competitor was on the red team, a boy who attended an art school. We checked on each other's progress, and I gloated when he began to look nervous. My opponent decided to take the creative route. He layered streaks of colors over each other, which ended up creating a thick, muddy background. In the end, he gave up and placed down two red handprints. We were sitting, facing each other on the bench where he was painting. I smiled at him and told him we'd already won. Then we stood up to see the Apache racers flying by. It was a camp-wide relay race with fifty activities. It ended as the team captains raced up the steps, past the art barn, to the Head Cabin. I cheered as the blue team won yet another competition.

The blue team won all of Maccabiah, the first time in my whole camp experience. My opponent on the red team picked me up and twirled me. A week or two later, I had my first kiss at three in the morning, in the darkness, sitting on my mattress in the corner of the bunk. My bed was at the front of the bunk, next to the door, but my friend let me switch our mattresses. The counselors were asleep, but they encouraged the boys to sneak in at night. They had all been campers too.

There was also a Judaica cabin, where our counselors talked to us about Judaism, and we watched documentaries like *Paper Clips*. This was the most boring part of camp. My Daled summer, I decided to fast on the Tisha B'Av, the anniversary of the destruction of the second temple. I think I had read somewhere that fasting was good for your health, but I told myself I was being a good, if not healthy, Jew.

It was hot as a group of us gathered in a cabin, surrounded by blankets and books. One girl told me that she planned to sneak out and drink water. I was reading *1984* and finished it. We played card games and talked, lying on our blankets on the sandy floor. We learned that a camping trip was leaving that night, one I had wanted to attend. We talked about how unfair it was to schedule a camping trip on a Jewish holiday. We were being punished for being good Jews, and wasn't that ironic? In the afternoon, I took a nap and woke up dizzy. I went outside and was told to lie back down. We broke the fast at sundown with bagels and granola bars.

Camp was coming to an end. On the last night, we decided to stay up and meet the boys in the field at midnight. Counselors caught us and sent us back inside. We sobbed together, and I fell asleep sideways on my friends' bed. We woke up at six thirty. We had set an alarm because our counselors always forgot to wake us. My first kiss, the first person I liked who liked me back, was sleeping inside the dining hall, where he was a waiter for that day. I hugged him and the rest of my friends. Then, we climbed inside the bus heading for the airport, with the promise that I would come back next year for the Israel trip. Nothing seemed more important than camp, then having fun, making memories. I never saw them again.

There's a sermon my rabbi tells during the major holidays. Last Yom Kippur, he stood at the bema and told us that we were disappearing. Less than .2% of the world is Jewish, and the numbers are declining as more Jews stop practicing and marry non-Jews. He begged us to raise our children Jewish.

Our rabbi's predictions are coming true. My brother, who attends a secular private school, is

Culture Shock

fourteen and a staunch atheist. He can't wait until he turns eighteen, when he can move out and stop keeping kosher. He feels only pressure to practice because of his heritage, which he cannot control. In his eyes, the world would be less violent without religion. My sister, on the other hand, attends a Jewish high school, where she has tests on how to keep Shabbat. Maybe religion is a way to build communities and bring families together, but it can also make people sheltered. If she had a choice, she wouldn't choose to be Jewish. She wouldn't choose any religion. But since religion exists, she practices Judaism because she knows the importance of keeping her family together. She knows her ancestors struggled, but she must go to synagogue, study Judaism, marry Jewish, for the sake of a religion to which she feels forcibly connected. In her school, the Bible is fed to her as fact, without room for interpretation or her own opinions. My siblings have given some thought to their place in Judaism, and their views are shared by many other young Jews.

    We are the next generation. Non-Jews, by no fault of their own, tend not to understand the breadth and reach of Jewish tradition, but we are under constant pressure to preserve our religion. In high school, my mother dated a boy from school who was Lebanese and Christian. She spent a lot of time with his family, who were nice to her, but his mother tried to convert her. She often said things like "Why can't you believe in Jesus Christ?" which made my mother uncomfortable.

My mother knew that her grandfather feared for his life in Austria. He was forced to flee after facing persecution for being Jewish. He became distrustful of non-Jews and frowned upon my mother having non-Jewish friends, let alone a non-Jewish boyfriend. It was important to my grandparents that my mother marry Jewish, and she didn't want to let down her family. All her life, it had been ingrained in her to maintain a Jewish household. She had imagined marrying a Jewish man and sending her children to Jewish Day School. She felt wrong dating her boyfriend because he wasn't Jewish. There was no place for him in her future. When she went away to college, she broke up with him.

My parents had told me, in what I thought was a joking tone, that I wasn't allowed to date people who weren't Jewish. When I returned home after my Daled summer, I felt infinitely older and more confident. Soon, I was back to running on the cross country team, catching my friends up on my summer, going to the state fair, finishing up my summer work. One thing was different. I was asked to homecoming, something I had never considered happening to me. I told my dad when he picked me up from school.

"That's great," my dad said. "Is he Jewish?"

"No," I said.

"We're going to have to talk about this later," my dad said. It was a reaction I hadn't been expecting. In the end, my parents decided I couldn't go with him. They wanted me to end up marrying someone Jewish, so they didn't want me to put myself in a position where I might marry someone else. I should just not date non-Jews, so I didn't have to make any hard decisions. What if I fell in love?

I was fifteen years old and had never had a boyfriend. Here was a boy I liked who gave me that chance to experience being a teenager. I wrote my parents a long heartfelt note, meant for them to read on Thanksgiving, because I thought it would put them in a forgiving mood. They found out the day before when my secret date hugged me at a school event.

My dad drove me home and asked if there was anything more than friendship between him and me.

"Let's listen to some music, " I said. We didn't talk. When we got home, I asked my parents to wait in their room while I came downstairs slowly with the letter. I ran inside, handed one copy to my dad and one to my mom, and made them promise not to start reading it until after I had left the room. A few minutes later, they called me back downstairs. They said they didn't hate me. They wouldn't forbid me from dating him, but they weren't going to encourage it.

To avoid encouraging the relationship, they made it difficult for me to see him outside of school. They wouldn't drive me to his house. His mother picked me up and drove me back home. They accused me of "baiting and switching" them because I had asked to attend a dance concert and didn't mention that he would also be in attendance. They didn't let me go. They brought the relationship up whenever they were upset with me. The fear of asking if I could see him made me scared to ask my parents for anything at all.

Once I was invited to a birthday party, which my parents did not want me to attend because he was going. The day of the party, we took a family trip to Washington D.C. On a tour of the White House, my father criticized the Christmas decorations. I told him that he was being disrespectful. That must have annoyed him, because as a protest for the deaths of Michael Brown and Eric Garner went past on the next street, my father was reminded of his recent visit to Boston, saying, "There an anti-Israel protest. You would have loved it, Elana."

I became upset, but he wouldn't apologize.

"Do you really want your daughter upset with you for the rest of the day," my mother said.

He kept walking. "Does she really want me to be upset with her for the rest of the year?" We walked into Corner Bakery, and I started sobbing in front of the cash register.

They let me go to the party and agreed to pick me up when it was over. I hugged him, left the warm room and entered the cold, silent car. A few days later, my father left for a business trip. When he returned, we embraced and didn't speak of the incident in Washington.

In the spring, the relationship ended, as most high school relationships tend to do, especially when there's an inconvenience. My mother gave me a hug and my father, who was away, called me to talk about coping with break-ups. Throughout the next summer, I experienced random surges of anger, in which I would burst into tears and criticize their treatment of me. Sometimes, these occurred in public places. My parents claimed that they hadn't been mean. Even now, it's a touchy subject. Once my sister and I were in an argument after I claimed that the students at her school were more sheltered than public school students.

"At least Mom and Dad can't hate me for dating someone not Jewish," my sister said.

"They didn't hate me," I said. I looked to my mother, who was standing with us in the kitchen. She didn't respond.

My parents told me that they wanted me to be happy, but they couldn't set aside their own feelings about me dating a non-Jew. Some things cross the line. I had been taught at my Jewish Day School that Judaism was about building walls, to create so many restrictions that one couldn't accidently break a law. For example, we keep kosher because the bible said not to eat a calf in its mother's milk, and we don't even want to get close to accidently doing that. I am only allowed to date Jewish so that I have no chance of marrying someone who isn't Jewish.

I told myself I would never date a non-Jewish person again because losing my parents over a boy wasn't worth it. I assumed that sacrifice was necessary to keep alive the memory of my ancestors who gave up everything to give me the opportunity to practice

Judaism. My life, and my love, will be temporary. I wish I believed this whole-heartedly, but as hard as I try, I can't. I threw out the letter I had written to my parents about love and religion and the meaning of life and didn't save a draft on my computer. I remember writing that I did not want to be part of a community that prevented people from loving who they chose or controlled what they believed in. If I deny myself love, it will be out of survivor's guilt.

Maybe I am selfish, but from the perspective of a daughter who felt lost, I wish my parents had supported me. I wish we hadn't felt cold to each other, and I wish I didn't feel guilty for disappointing them.

Balancing happiness and modernity with tradition is one of the fundamental conflicts of Judaism. When Chava marries Fyedka in *Fiddler on the Roof,* Tevye proclaims her dead to him. Chava begs him to accept the marriage. He turns away from her and ponders, "Can I deny everything I believe in? On the other hand, can I deny my own daughter? On the other hand, how can I turn my back on my faith, my people? If I try and bend that far, I'll break." He disowns her and mourns.

Every year I notice that Passover changes. Of course, the order itself is the same, as we follow the Haggadah. But a seder is made up of people, and we tend to change quite a bit.

Yoni is no longer eight, Ari is not seven, I am not six, and Liyat is not five. The twins and Elan are

Culture Shock

not infants. The oldest of my aunt's three little girls just had her Bat Mitzvah. We don't meet in that log cabin in Gatlingburg with a creek in the back, spending the days hiking, picking flowers, wrestling, and drying our shoes in the microwave.

We are in Silver Spring, seated around three tables pushed together, covered with four tablecloths, an arrangement we had helped set up that morning. The seders do not feel like six hours, and the food does not come after we have been starving, rationing our cucumbers and matzah. The children do not leave the table after dinner, escaping upstairs in Bubbe and Zayde's house, the log cabin, or the basement in my home. My cousin does not pretend to kidnap Liyat and me. We are not princesses. We don't wear silky pink dresses with flowers. We pull on our skirts to keep them from riding up our thighs. We complain that the food is tasteless and that matzah gives us constipation. The night does not have a quality that without a doubt, this night is different from all other nights.

Somehow, there have always been more or less twenty-seven of us. Before there were the girls, there was Yussel and Manny and their wives, and the whole table felt miles long and foreign. When I recited the Ma Nishtana, I was terrified, my eyes trained on Zayde as he nodded with encouragement. Then he and Yussel lead *Ehad Mi'Yodaia,* "Who knows one?" and the seders would run too late in loud, chaotic song, never in tune. Now Zayde cannot sing Ehad Mi'Yodaia because Yussel is not here to help him lead.

He looks tired. He and Bubbe do not sit at the head of the table. After the final chorus of *Had Gadya*, "One Little Goat," and *Chasal Siddur* Pesach, "The Seder Has Ended," we break up the seder and help clean up. We hug our cousins good-bye until the next year. There is no gathering around the piano for songs, like we used to when my father kept "The Jewish Fake Book" on the music stand. We load the car, while my mother complains that it took us too long to leave. We see lights flicker in the window, next to Zayde sitting in the armchair, lost in thought.

SJH: Crusades to Ottoman Empire

- In 1099, the Crusaders come from Europe to recover the Holy Land. In the First Crusade, knights capture Jerusalem, massacring most non-Christians. Barricaded in their synagogues, the Jews defend their quarter. The Crusaders become forceful. Jews are either burned to death or sold into slavery.
- Through treaties, agreements, and bloody battles, the Crusaders gain power over all of the land. They open transportation routes from Europe, pilgrimages become a pastime, and Jews try to return home. Three hundred rabbis from France and England settle in Akko and Jerusalem.
- Under the sultan Saladin, a Muslim army overthrows the Crusaders and gives Jews the right to live in Jerusalem again. In 1291, the Mamluks, a Muslim military class from Egypt, defeat the Crusaders for good. In fear, they destroy all ports besides Damascus, Akko, and Yafo. This ends up interrupting maritime and overland commerce, ruining urban centers, leaving Jerusalem abandoned.

- By the end of the Middle Ages, the Jewish community in the land is diminished and poverty stricken. The people grow restless. At the same time, locusts invade crop fields and frequent earthquakes rattle the earth.
- Then, the Black Death hits Europe in 1348. Families watch as purple lumps cover their loved ones. The dead pile up on the streets. The Jews, who bathe in the Mikvah on the Sabbath, do not get sick, so they are blamed for the plague.
- In 1492, following expulsion from Spain, many Jews return to Israel. In the Jewish town of Safed (Tzfat), the population rises to 10,000 and the town becomes a textile center.
- In 1517, the Ottomans conquer and divide the land into four districts. Kabbalah, the study of Jewish mysticism, becomes popular. The *Shulhan Arukh*, a codification of Jewish law, spreads throughout the Diaspora.

On Stories

> "That's what fiction is for. It's for getting at the truth when the truth isn't sufficient for the truth."
> —Tim O'Brien

Sometimes, essays begin with an anecdote about a relevant topic to hook the reader:

    During Passover one year, when we still celebrated at my grandparents' house in Nashville, my cousins and I left dinner to play. I stood at the bottom of the staircase, playing catch with my cousin, who stood at the top. Back and forth, we threw my sister's stuffed puppy, until I lost aim and knocked a picture off the wall. My cousin picked up the dog, and we went downstairs, tails between our legs, to tell Bubbe. I felt my throat close up as I tried to prevent myself from crying in front of the whole family. I cried anyway. Bubbe took my hand, brought me upstairs, put the picture back on the wall, and told me everything was okay. I sat back in my seat, deciding not to play for the rest of the seder, and my throat hurt for the rest of the night. After a few days, the pain had increased, and the doctor diagnosed me with strep throat. There has probably never been a proven correlation between stress and strep throat, and my mom made the argument that I had spent days playing with ten other young children who could have been carrying the infection, but I became convinced that my fear had made me sick.

Sometimes the story isn't interesting or relevant enough to keep people reading. In this case, the author realizes that the essay is not about Passover, infections, or fear, but rather about the technique of storytelling. Let's try a different anecdote:

Krieger Schechter Day School held a Scholastics book fair every year. One of the auditoriums was converted into a bookstore, and tables were carried in, along with shelves of hundreds and hundreds of books. While my class waited our turn outside, we could guess how many candies were in a jar and win if we got closest to the correct amount. (I guessed every year. I didn't win the candy until I was in seventh grade, by averaging out everyone else's guesses, but that's not really relevant either). Finally, the doors opened, and we ran inside. The volunteers gave us wish lists for our parents and instructions that we never heard because the books were calling us, luring us close with whispers of adventure, and if we were lucky, the secrets of life. I had a hard time squeezing all the titles I wanted onto the wish list.

In second grade, I requested a version of Cinderella and handed my list to my mom before she left to pick up our books. Instead, she came home with a book called *Charlotte's Web*. As I pouted, she told me, "You've read Cinderella so many times. This was one of my favorite books growing up."

Charlotte's Web sat in my drawer for a few more months. I didn't want to read a book about a pig or the pensive girl on the cover. Finally, when there was nothing else to read, I picked it up, and something strange happened. Suddenly, I wasn't in my living room anymore. I was on a farm, swinging on ropes in the barn with my brother, and nursing a runty pig back to health. And then I was taking mud baths in the Zuckerman farm and feeling horrible loneliness every night, trying to sleep on an empty stomach, and getting saved by a spider.

When I finished the book, my world was torn apart. I knew stories had happy endings. I knew Wilbur wasn't going to be eaten. But E.B. White had never shown an indication that Charlotte was in danger of dying, and I felt completely betrayed. I wasn't hopeful when Charlotte's three daughters came back to Wilbur. Charlotte was gone. I watched the 1973 movie with my family and missed the ending again because I couldn't see the screen through my tears.

I learned the hard way that stories don't always have happy endings. In time, I came to suspect happy endings of cheating. Real stories were much more complicated.

Elana Rubin

In seventh grade, I began to read *The Once and Future King*, which details the life of King Arthur, drawing the sword from the stone, trained by Merlin, married to the beautiful Guinevere, who is having a torrid love affair with Sir Lancelot. It was all so exciting. I sat on the front porch sipping iced tea as Sir Galahad galloped home clutching the Holy Grail. The crusades were a thing of mythology, far removed, an adventure. King Arthur emerges as a force of goodness in an amoral society. In the end, he cannot defeat evil. He is overpowered by Might, betrayed by his vengeful son, and corruption once again takes hold of England. He remembers the island where puffins, razorbills, guillemots, and kittiwakes lived peacefully and "saw the problem before him as plain as a map. The fantastic thing about war was that it was fought about nothing—literally nothing. Frontiers were imaginary lines." He calls on a page to keep his story alive, so truth and his ideals would be preserved. I finished the book late one night when I was supposed to be sleeping. Satisfied with a bittersweet ending and the twisting in my stomach, the feeling of reading something powerful, I closed the book and set it on my bedside table. I went to the bathroom to brush my teeth.

Some part of me knew that the Crusades had happened, but I never placed King Arthur in the timeline of history. Stories were just stories, from which I could not pull out the thread of reality. In Jewish history class, we acted out the Spanish

Inquisition. We laughed as our classmates forced us out of Spain, sentenced us to death, or if we were lucky enough, brought us into hiding as Marranos, lighting Shabbat candles in our basement.

I knew that there had been an Inquisition, but I'm not sure when I started realizing that these events actually *happened*. At some point, I gained the ability to place history in the context of my life. These were people who had actually lived, and my life is built on the foundations of the expulsions and injustices the Jews experienced.

There is no truth in textbooks. I can sit at my computer and type out Some Jewish History sections, but they don't reveal what these times were really like. I didn't understand history until I decided to look into the life of one of its characters. I watched a young Jewish man from the Middle Ages eating, sleeping, dreaming, falling in love, dying. I read his mind, his irrational fear of his back door, which is at the end of the hall and too dark to see at night. I sink my teeth into the warm bread he eats, feel his cool tears as his mind wanders to memories of his mother when he can't fall asleep, the lines on his hands, the nervous spasm of his big toe.

I still remember the most vivid images from books I read as a child. In first grade, I read a historical fiction book about the Revolutionary War, and I still wince at the descriptions of the soldier's bloody tracks in the snow. In the first book I couldn't bring myself to finish, a girl gets hit by a car, which slices off her pinkie toe. The man who hit her brings cashews to the hospital because they look like pinkie toes. "Do not go gentle into that good night"… "What light through yonder window breaks?"…"They is, they is, they is." These are the stories that stay with me. When there is nothing else to hold onto, when nothing else makes sense, these stories are my comfort.

Perhaps closer to the end of the essay, the author realizes the point of writing, discovers the hidden call beneath the clumsy lines, constructed in the dark beside a low glass of water. Once the author finds the point, the essay culminates in a final, powerful anecdote:

The girl is a compulsive truth teller. In fourth grade, she exchanges emails with a camp friend, who signs one correspondence, "your best friend." After staring for a few minutes in panic, the girl decides her friend should be corrected.

"You're not my best friend," she writes. "I already have one." This is the first friend she loses.

It's not that big of a deal though. There are other friends, and there are also books, which are often more entertaining. She's reading *The Magic Tree House* books, about Jack and Annie, who travel to different periods of history in a magic tree house. They visit Japan and learn the art of poetry. They visit Hawaii and learn the meaning of friendship. They travel to Venice and save the city from a flood, all of this with wide eyes and deep understanding of the human condition. Then, they return home and go

Culture Shock

back to whatever they were doing before solving the world's major problems.

She wants to solve problems too. She promises God that if He makes her a writer, she will expose ignorance. She wants to publish a book by the time she is thirteen and appear on Ellen and become famous.

This does not happen. Instead, she applies to a magnet art high school. A few years older, she doubts her talent. She knows she is not good enough to get in, but she is accepted and takes her first steps toward a writing career. In her freshman year, her class is given the task of peeling an onion painfully slowly, allowing the thin wrinkled layers to fall on their desks, their eyes to tear, and their hands to smell like onions for the rest of the day. She works through the Styrofoam-like midsection until she reaches the small bulb-like center. Inside, it is hollow, with vein-like sectors flowing through passages like the human heart.

She never loses sight of the "plan," though she's not quite sure what "exposing ignorance" means. She narrows it down to a specific goal of writing for a purpose. Instead of fighting ignorance, she lays down her armor and tells the truth. If exposing ignorance is too vague an ambition, the exact opposite is cold hard fact.

Or is it? It doesn't take her too long to realize that facts can be interpreted in so many different ways, that they end up meaning nothing at all. How much of the truth can be absorbed from the description of Joan of Arc's martyrdom in a textbook without hearing the fire crackling beneath her, smelling the smoke, reading her most intimate thoughts at that moment? How much truth can be taken from the broadcast of an accident on the highway without knowing the man who was killed, having grown up with him, attended his wedding, seen him unemployed, curled up on the floor of a motel room, seen him fight through rapids in a bad riptide? How much truth exists in the headline: "6 Palestinian Teens Die Amid Mideast Unrest," without knowing that these teenagers were shot in Jerusalem while stabbing an ultra-Orthodox Jew and two Israeli police officers?

By now, she has learned that her writing will never be good enough. Perhaps this essay was about fear after all. She wants to write with no ulterior motive but to reveal the truth, but she fears getting the truth wrong. The only way to write about truth is to tell her truth. She cannot write about her experiences in Israel without writing about Israel, and she cannot write about Israel without writing about the inevitable elephant in the room: conflict. Jewish and Israeli history is riddled with conflict.

She learns that a lack of perfection will not make her writing insignificant, without the purpose part of the "plan." There is strength in her inability, the human necessity in addressing conflict the only way she knows how: through stories. She will start from the outer layer and peel. Deeper and deeper. And maybe we can make sense of things.

SJH: First Aliyah to White Papers

- In 1882, following pogroms in Russia, nearly 35,000 Jews from Eastern Europe immigrate to Ottoman Palestine. This becomes known as the first Aliyah, or large scale immigration.
- In 1894, a Jewish captain of the French army, Alfred Dreyfus, is falsely accused of providing Germany with military secrets. He is found guilty of treason and sentenced to prison for life. A public ceremony is held in Paris, where Dreyfus is paraded before a crowd shouting "Death to the Jew."
- In 1897, Austro-Hungarian journalist Theodor Herzl holds the first Zionist Congress in Basel, Switzerland. He argues for the founding of a Jewish homeland in the Holy Land.
- In 1917, Great Britain conquers Palestine, ending 400 years of Ottoman rule. More immigrants settle in Palestine, from Russia, Poland, and Germany.
- In 1922, the British gain the Mandate for Palestine by the League of Nations, recognizing, "the historical connection of the Jewish people with Palestine." In charge of

establishing a Jewish homeland, Great Britain and the League of Nations forbid Jews from settling in Transjordan, three-fourths of the Mandate. This leaves one fourth of the land for the Jewish national home.

- The Jewish community, aware of how things usually go, establishes the Jewish Agency to represent them and connect Jewish communities to the goal of a Jewish state. It helps people make Aliyah and builds towns and villages in the Mandate.
- In 1929, after disputes about the rights of Jews to pray at the Western Wall, Arab militants riot in Hebron. Jews are massacred, ending a period of relative peace.
- The British White Papers of 1930, by Colonel Secretary Lord Passfield, restrict immigration and acquisition of land by Jews.
- In 1931, under Arab pressure, the British government withdraws from preserving the Mandate. Irgun, the Jewish underground organization, is founded.
- In 1936, fearing a large Arab riot, the Jewish community in Palestine, called the Yishuv, meets with the British Deputy High Commissioner. The British officials assure them that the government "will take care of it." The government does not "take care of it." The next day, riots break out against Jews. They continue for three years.

- In 1939, further White Papers declare that Palestine will be an independent state, neither Jewish nor Arab. Jewish immigration is limited to 75,000 for the first five years and will later be dependent upon Arab consent.

A Body of Land

To Jewish children, Israel seems like a fantasy land, where dreams come true, and manna, in the form of pita and falafel, falls from heaven. Israel was like Disney World but better, before we found out that Walt Disney was anti-Semitic and it's impossible to get on a ride without a FastPass. In kindergarten, we looked at large laminated maps of Israel and a picture of a man reading a newspaper on the Dead Sea. We learned the names of cities: Tel Aviv, Eilat, Haifa, and most importantly, Jerusalem. Jerusalem was *it,* where every important historical event took place, where history would continue, and where we would end up, when the mysterious Messiah we were starting to hear about finally came. If someone told me the bricks of Jerusalem were made of gold bars, I would have believed it.

I visited Israel for the first time when I was seven years old. That morning, I woke up and jumped out of bed, begging my family to hurry to the airport. We weren't as close to Israel as I thought. We waited as my parents checked our luggage, then waited as we went through security. When we landed, we were only in Newark and had to wait at the gate for our flight to

Culture Shock

Israel. Although my parents had spoken to me about the twelve-hour flight, it was much longer in real time. I watched some movies, tried to sleep, slept for a few minutes until I was awakened by the smell of scrambled eggs being served under my nose. When we landed in the Ben Gurion airport, the passengers clapped and sang "Hevenu Shalom Alechem." When we arrived at the hotel, I was in a much better mood.

Even in a country the size of New Jersey, two weeks in Israel is barely enough time to see the major sites. We visited Tel-Aviv and bought falafel off the street, crunchy and dripping with creamy tahini, enveloped in a warm fluffy pita. Cars zipped on the street, bright lights weaved through the city, and Israeli music somehow harmonized with the hum of accelerating cars and screeching of abrupt braking. In the crowded Carmel Market, we held hands to avoid being separated and took in the smell of bright spices, red and yellow in color, and sweat. There were vats of steamed corn and fresh squeezed lemonade, orange juice, pomegranate juice, carrot juice, anything that could be juiced. We bought dried strawberries, which the vendor scooped out from a large mound surrounded by candies, nuts, apricots, and bright green pineapple. Every salesperson hollered at us to buy jewelry, offering to lower the price by five shekels, no ten shekel, he'd give it to us for fifteen. You'd never get a deal like it anywhere else! In the next stall, the vendor yelled the same thing. My sister and I covered our noses with our shirts as we passed the fresh fish and cow carcass hanging from the ceiling.

Outside the market, we breathed and the breeze relieved our dripping backs. There was a craft festival every Tuesday and Thursday on Nahalat Binyamin Street, where artists sold paintings, gem-encrusted earrings, hand-dipped scarves, intricate puppets, and customizable yarmulkes. My parents let each of us buy one object. I chose a hedgehog stuffed animal and named it Nahalat Binyamin.

We drove to Jerusalem. Approaching the Western Wall, we split, men in one section, women in the other. My mother, sister, and I went to the bathroom to change into long skirts. The women wore shawls and skirts to their ankles, despite the Middle Eastern heat, rocking back and forth as they prayed, pressing their foreheads to the holy wall. They kissed it. They stuck notes between cracks in the limestone. Their daughters pressed against the *mechitza*[1] and watched their brothers and fathers standing tall in their black hats. We regretted not bringing any paper.

We drove to the Dead Sea, the lowest point on land, more than 400 meters below sea level. My ears popped as we descended towering, sloping sand dunes. My father explained that thousands of years ago, all of our surroundings had been underwater. We came to a rocky patch on the edge of the water. I had a cut on my

---

[1] A permanent prayer barrier separating men and women at the Western Wall

Culture Shock

finger and didn't want to go in because I knew the salt would sting. I watched my family floating on the surface of the waves and wished I had the courage to go in. After they dried off, we visited the cool museum, dimly lit to preserve the ancient writing of the Dead Sea Scrolls, which had been found in 1946 by a shepherd following a lost sheep. Now the Dead Sea is disappearing. It's supposed to dry out by 2050.

I was not too young to miss the soldiers on the street in full uniform, rifles strapped to their backs. There was immense, overwhelming beauty in the land, but there was ugliness too. On our way back to Tel Aviv from Jerusalem, we also accidently drove through the West Bank. Suddenly all the signs on storefronts turned to Arabic. Men in turbans shouted to one another. My father gripped the wheel and told everyone to be quiet so he could concentrate. After a few minutes, we found an exit and my parents relaxed. I didn't know my parents could be afraid of anything, but I felt their fear intensely in those few minutes. I noticed my heart beating fast.

In our year in Tel Aviv, we woke up early on Saturday, grabbed our bikes, and headed to the Tayelet, or the boardwalk, to buy fresh produce from the market. We passed waves and teenagers playing soccer on the beach. A group of fit middle-aged men and women danced traditional Israeli dances in the square, turning in circles, spinning, meeting in the center, and stepping gracefully in a grapevine. We stopped to watch my grandmother, who knew every step. At night, couples embraced along the ocean shore, stars above them. Boys played footvolley under the lights. A street performer strummed the guitar. The palm trees hung over the sandy pavement. The air smelled of salt and life.

We took a tour of the Western Wall Tunnels. On the descent, my father and sister became claustrophobic. I'd never had this problem, but I practiced breathing exercises. I listened to the guide point out the different layers of the wall made from different materials throughout history. We arrived to the closest spot to the Holy of Holies, where it was believed that God dwelt in the tabernacle. Religious Jews were deep in prayer, so the guide whispered. Prayer books lined the wall. I've never felt religious, but there was an old and powerful feeling in those tunnels, almost mystical. I would not have been surprised to see ancient Jerusalem when I emerged from the tunnels.

The same year, my cousin Ari had his Bar Mitzvah at the Western Wall. All of the women stood on chairs to see the service over the mechitza. A woman frowned at us and told us to get down. She tried to give a shawl to my cousin's Israeli grandmother, who was secular and insisted on wearing a sleeveless shirt and slacks. As the services ended, we flooded from the Wall with hundreds of other Jews.

Culture Shock

When Mark Twain came to Israel, the land looked much different. He recounted his experiences in his book *Innocents Abroad*:

> We pressed on toward the goal of our crusade, renowned Jerusalem. The further we went the hotter the sun got and the more rocky and bare, repulsive and dreary the landscape became... There was hardly a tree or a shrub anywhere. Even the olive and the cactus, those fast friends of a worthless soil, had almost deserted the country. No landscape exists that is more tiresome to the eye than that which bounds the approaches to Jerusalem... Jerusalem is mournful, dreary and lifeless. I would not desire to live here. It is a hopeless, dreary, heartbroken land... Palestine sits in sackcloth and ashes.

The Israeli terrain used to be rocky, filled with swamps and dust and rough plants. The first Jewish immigrants were idealists who were trying to trade a hopeless life for a hopeful one. They knew nothing about agriculture but decided to form *moshavot*, or farming villages. They faced extreme heat, sand storms, dehydration, and disease. They dealt with Turkish taxes and Arab opposition with barely any financial aid or skill with a plow. They planted eucalyptus trees from Australia to drain swamps, reducing mosquitos and the spread of Malaria.

Even in kindergarten, when we were introduced to Israel for the first time, emphasis was placed on the idea of building. We sang ,"Eretz Yisrael sheli yafah vegam porachat, mi banah umi nata? Kulanu beyachad!" "My land of Israel is beautiful and flourishing. Who built and who planted it? We all did together!" Forming a roof with our hands, we sang, "I built a house in the land of Israel. So we have the land and we have a house in the land of Israel." By the end of the song, we had the land, a house, a tree, a road, a bridge, and a song about Israel. In HaZamir, we sing "Zum Gali Gali," the song the pioneers sang as they worked: "Hechalutz lema'an avodah avodah lema'an hechalutz." "The pioneer is meant for work, work is meant for the pioneer." The nation is built from their hands. It flows with their sweat, backbreaking, raw-handed labor.

To combat anti-Semitism in the nineteenth century, writer Theodore Herzl imagined a socialist utopian Jewish society in the land of Israel.[2] He called a congress in Switzerland to discuss the establishment of a Jewish homeland. Eventually, there were twelve Zionist Congresses. Uganda was considered as a temporary refuge for Jews, but ultimately the Uganda Plan was rejected, and the focus of Zionism remained, as the delegates of the Zionist Congress declared, "to

---

[2] He wrote a book about it: *Altneuland,* or *Old New Land.*

establish a home for the Jewish people in Palestine secured under public law." The Second Aliyah, or wave of immigration, was composed of Russian Jews fleeing programs. Inspired by the idea of a utopian society, they set up the first kibbutz, Degania Alef, in 1909.

By the time the British conquered Palestine, there were forty-four Jewish settlements in the land. In the Third and Fourth Aliyot, Russian, Polish, and Hungarian Jews escaped persecution in Israel. Unlike the Aliyot before, these immigrants were middle class families. In Palestine, they established small businesses, balancing an economy that had been dependent on agriculture.

In 1917, the British Foreign Secretary wrote the Balfour Declaration, pledging to support the establishment of a "Jewish national home in Palestine." A year before, the British had struck a deal with France to divide the land among themselves. They also promised the ruler of Mecca, Sarif Hussein, that he would rule over an Arab state in Palestine if he led an Arab revolt against the Ottoman Empire. When the Ottoman Empire fell, the British gained victory and the other parties gained empty promises. Hussein's sons were allowed to rule under British protection. Prince Faisal became king of Iraq and Syria, and Prince Abdullah was made king of Jordan. However, the real authority was in the hands of the British and French.

The largest Aliyah took place after the Nazis took over Germany. Almost a quarter of a million Jews moved to Palestine. These were professionals, such as doctors, lawyers, scientists, and artists. Jews were allowed to settle in Palestine; however, to avoid angering Arabs, the British placed quotas on the number that could enter. Jews tried to immigrate illegally, which did anger the Arabs, who thought the land to be theirs. The modern Israeli Palestinian conflict is not a thousand year old religious feud, but a battle over the rights to land. The borders between Arab countries were created arbitrarily by European colonizers to divide people against one another.

Jerusalem is the sacred site of the Abrahamic religions. For Jews, Jerusalem is the capital of the ancient kingdom, where the Western Wall, the only remains of the temples, stands. For Christians, Jerusalem is the site of Jesus's crucifixion and resurrection. For Muslims, the Prophet Muhammad was transported to Jerusalem on his journey to heaven. Today, Jerusalem is a place of conflict.

In the original 1947 partition plan, the United Nations General Assembly voted to split Palestine into Jewish and Arab States, with Jerusalem as an international, autonomous city. After the War of Independence, East and West Jerusalem were separated by barbed wire and land mines, with Palestinians residing in East Jerusalem and Jewish citizens staying in West Jerusalem. When Jerusalem was reunified during the Six-Day War, Israel offered citizenships to the Palestinians living there. They declined, believing that accepting would be submission

Culture Shock

to Israeli rule. They also believed that Jerusalem might one day become the capital of a Palestinian state.

After Israel gained control of East Jerusalem, it upheld that non-Muslims could visit the Temple Mount but were prohibited from praying there. This ban was often violated during Jewish holidays. Provoked by Jewish visits, Muslim Palestinians believed that the Israeli government was working to allow Jewish prayer. The Israeli government denied these claims.

Prayer, however, is not the largest source of tension in Jerusalem. Jewish residents of Jerusalem are citizens of Israel, while Palestinians are permanent residents, with Israeli IDs. More than 300,000 Arabs live in East Jerusalem. They receive government benefits and have voting rights but reject any role in politics. If Palestinians leave Jerusalem for seven years, Israel maintains the right to take away their residency permit. On the other hand, in the West Bank, one area is controlled by the Palestinian Authority[3], one is under complete Israeli control, and one is under joint control. Arab residents can enter all three, but Jewish citizens are barred from entering the area administered by the Palestinian Authority by a large sign that says, "It is forbidden for Israeli citizens to enter." Once two Israeli soldiers accidentally entered a city in the area. They were caught and lynched. Other

---

[3] The interim government body formed in 1994 by the Oslo Accords

Jewish residents, who made a wrong turn or tried to visit, have been turned over to the police.

At the end of eighth grade, I returned to Israel on a school trip. I was excited to spend ten days with my friends, exploring and shopping, hiking and eating Israeli food. Unexpectedly, I was struck with strong nostalgia and wrote poetry nearly the entire plane ride. When we landed, my friend, who had never been to Israel before, began to cry. Throughout the trip, I continued to scribble in my journal. I felt inspired everywhere I went. Ideas flooded faster than I could put them down. We visited Mount Herzl Cemetery, home to thousands of buried soldiers, with yellow tulips on their headstones, photographs and Israeli flags planted in the soil. We visited Yad Vashem, the Holocaust museum. I wrote poems with lines like "our red faces breathe life between black eyes, glossy from film sheets."

My first trip, I had been too young, and my second trip, I had been too stubborn, but on the third trip, I saw the beauty of the land before me. At the very top of Israel are the Golan Heights, green and tan mountains overlooking valleys, square fields, the blue Kinneret like a gemstone set in undisturbed valleys, fields, and orchards. We stopped by the road where a robed Druze woman baked lafa on a dome-shaped oven, filling it with chocolate or oil and cheese. The coast is home to clear waves and smooth sands, dotted with markets selling bright red spices, roasted nuts,

Culture Shock

and intricate tapestries. The Negev is hot and dusty during the day, but at night it reaches cold temperatures. We rode camels along the sloping dunes, which spread for miles in every direction, and ate our fill of pita, hummus, roasted vegetables, rice with spices, baklava, and sweet tea in a Bedouin tent. We sat around a fire and hiked through the desert at night, leaning against rocks and looking up as if we existed in a snow globe where stars swirled instead of snow. Before sunrise, we climbed to the top of Masada and were retold the harrowing story of the Jewish rebels hiding in the fortress from the Romans. Although forbidden by Jewish law, all 960 of the rebels committed suicide as an alternative to slavery and prostitution by the Romans. We yelled off the edge of the mesa, "Am Yisrael Chai!"[4] and heard its reverberation call back to us before trailing into the wind.

In the Dead Sea, we covered ourselves with mud and floated despite the sting of salt. In Jerusalem, we walked on ancient limestone in long skirts, as traditional tunes swept in the wind from the bow of a street performer. We stood in a circle before the Western Wall and sang Hebrew songs as Israeli women joined us in the *horah*. In Eilat, bright lights filled the night like a carnival. We were sticky and sweaty and tired, but we did not want to sleep for fear of missing a moment. I accidentally bought too much

---

[4] A Jewish saying: "The People of Israel Live"

jewelry and dyed candles in the art village of Tzfat and spent the last of my shekels on a man with a sign that said his house had burned down.

Israel is a melting pot of culture. My family heard Hebrew, Polish, and Arabic in French-style cafes. In my class at the Ramat Aviv Gimel School, there was an Ethiopian boy named Thomas Edison. He spoke Amharic and was still learning Hebrew along with me, although he was grasping it more quickly than I was. There are more than 120,000 Ethiopian Jews living in Israel. In the 1980s, after a famine occurred in Ethiopia, Israel transported thousands of Ethiopian Jews to Israel by aircraft in a mission known as Operation Moses. In the 1990s, after Ethiopia's capital was captured by rebels, Operation Solomon transported 15,000 Ethiopian Jews to Israel. In 2010, 8,000 Falash Mura,[5] who had been living in transit camps in northern Ethiopia, migrated to Israel.

Israel is also home to other minorities, such as Samaritans, who have lived in Israel for 2,500 years, Orthodox Coptic Christians, Druze, and Bedouin. About 20 percent of the population is Arab, and 1.4 million Sunni Arabs live in Israel, mostly in the North, Jaffa, and Jerusalem. For the 16 percent of the population that is Muslim, Israel funds more than 100 public mosques, including the money necessary to purchase Korans and pay the salaries of imams, or

---

[5] Ethiopian Jews who had converted to Christianity to avoid persecution in the 1800s

religious leaders. The Israeli government also provides for Arab schools and Islamic schools and colleges. Israelis travel to East Jerusalem for less expensive shopping and services and hummus restaurants. Palestinians study at the Hebrew University, work, and go to bars in West Jerusalem. Major surgeries for both Palestinians and Israelis take place at Israeli hospitals.

On each of their holy days, Christians, Muslims, and Jews go to their sections to pray. It is not unusual to see different religions practicing side by side. I saw a picture of a Jew praying with a tallit and tefillin. Beside him, a Muslim kneeled barefoot on a carpet. A group called Praying Together holds interfaith events, in which Jewish, Muslims, and Christians learn from each other, pray alongside one another, and eat together. On these days, Jerusalem is all holiness. On the ancient streets, only song and sanctity exist.

SJH: Holocaust to Munich Olympics

- From 1939-1945, six million Jews, and eleven million people all together, are murdered in the Holocaust.
- In 1944, the Jewish Brigade is formed as part of British forces, trying to bring European Holocaust survivors to Palestine.
- In 1947, the United Nations proposes the establishment of Arab and Jewish states in Palestine, including breaking Jerusalem into three Jewish sections and four Arab sections, with international administration. Despite these limitations, the Jewish Agency for Palestine accepts the plan. Unwilling to accept any territorial division, the Arab nations oppose the plan and walk out of the General Assembly. Civil war breaks out in Palestine among Jewish and Arab communities.
- On May 14th, 1948, the British Mandate ends and Israel gains its independence with its first prime minister, David Ben-Gurion. On May 15th, Israel is invaded by five Arab nations in the War of Independence.

Culture Shock

- Ben-Gurion establishes the Israeli Defense Force as a unified force to protect Israel. Israel wins the war, gains much more land, and signs armistice agreements with Egypt, Jordan, Syria, and Lebanon. Jerusalem is divided between Israeli and Jordanian rule.
- During the First Arab-Israeli War, 700,000 Palestinians become refugees. One third go to the West Bank under Jordan's control, another third go to the Gaza strip controlled by Egypt, and the rest go to Jordan, Lebanon, and Syria. The Arab nations refuse to absorb the Palestinians and they are put in refugee camps. Only the King of Jordan agrees to consider giving them citizenship.
- In 1956, Egypt violates the terms of the armistice by closing the Suez Canal and the Straits of Tiran to Israeli shipping and imports. In the second Arab-Israeli war, the IDF, joined by Great Britain and France, captures the Gaza Strip and the Sinai Peninsula.
- In 1964, the National Water Carrier is complete, which brings water from Lake Kinneret in the north to the semi-arid south. The same year, the Palestine Liberation Organization forms, with the goal of achieving independence of political action from Arab regimes, liberating Palestine, and securing the return of refugees.

- In 1967, Egypt closes the Straits of Aqaba to Israeli shipping after the UN withdraws. The president declares his intention to annihilate the Jewish state and forges military alliances with Syria and Jordan, building up troop concentrations along the border with Israel and blocking shipping to Eilat.
- After Egypt, Syria, and Jordan form an alliance and mobilize troops along the border, Israel launches a preemptive strike. The Third Arab-Israeli war lasts only six days. Israel gains Judea, Samaria, Gaza, the Sinai Peninsula, and the Golan Heights.
- In 1969, provided with weapons by the Soviet Union, the Egyptians fire toward Israeli targets by the Suez Canal, and the Israeli Air Force attacks Egyptian army posts along the Canal. After Israeli pilots shoot down five Russian MiGs, Moscow pressures Egypt to agree to a ceasefire.
- In 1973, the Yom Kippur War occurs
- In 1974, the Arab league recognizes the Palestinian Liberation Organization (PLO), which sought to liberate Palestine by destroying Israel, as the legitimate representative of the Palestinian people.
- In 1978, the Camp David Accords plan for comprehensive peace in the Middle East and propose Palestinian self-government.

Culture Shock

- In 1978, after a PLO attack in Israel results in many dead and wounded, Israel invades Southern Lebanon. The Lebanese government protests to the UN Security Council, stating that it has no connection with the Palestinian operation. The Council calls on Israel to cease military action and withdraw forces.
- Israeli Prime Minister Menachem Begin and Egyptian President Anwar El-Sadat sign the Camp David Accords, a peace treaty between Israel and Egypt. Begin and Sadat win the Nobel Peace Prize.
- In 1979, Egypt is expelled from the Arab League for making peace with Israel. In 1981, Sadat is assassinated by Muslim extremists.
- In 1982, the Black September Movement, a band of Palestinian militants, murder eleven Israeli athletes at the Munich Olympics, demanding the release of more than 200 Palestinian guerillas held in Israeli jails.

Aliyah

Abba Rubin applied to one college because his guidance counselors were useless and his parents didn't know anything about college. This college was Columbia University. In his interview, he told the admissions officer about a play he wrote that was put on in Liberty. He knew it was an overly dramatic story, one guy killing another, but Columbia accepted him and offered him a full tuition scholarship of one thousand dollars.

He recalled this story with a chuckle and a comment on the cost of college tuition today. "They must've known I was going to meet your bubbe, and anyone who would meet her must be all right," he told me.

Carol Shames was spending a week at the Stevensville Hotel in the Catskills with her mother. The waiter at their table was a charming law student named Yussel Rubin. He was smitten with Carol, but she was only fifteen years old, so he asked to introduce

Culture Shock

her to his brother Abba. Carol's mother liked and trusted Yussel, so she let her daughter go.

Yussel borrowed a car from a friend to take Carol to Liberty, which was just a few miles away. The car had a faulty clutch and drove with jerky motions, and Carol, who was usually not nervous in cars, clung to her seat, until she reached the Rubin's house and could step out of the car. They rang the doorbell, and Abba answered wearing only boxer shorts. Carol was embarrassed to look at him, and Abba showed even less interest. He went into another room, leaving Carol and Yussel in the living room to entertain themselves. There was a fair in town that Yussel had hoped Abba would take Carol to. Abba said that she was too young, so Carol went with Yussel, leaving Abba in the house.

Yussel lived in Boston, while Columbia was only four subway stops from Carol's house. On Carol's sixteenth birthday, she was having a party at her house with her friends when Yussel called to say that he was in town and he and Abba wanted to come over. Carol tried to say no and tell them about the party, but her mother took the phone and invited them. Yussel came in, dragging Abba by the wrist. This broke up the party. There was lots of food left over and Carol's mother invited the boys to eat. Carol was annoyed that her party had been ruined.

Shortly after they left her house, Abba called and asked if Carol wanted to go out that night. She said she couldn't. It was her birthday, and she was seeing her sister. Two weeks later, he called again, and again, Carol was busy that night. He waited another two weeks before calling, once again inviting her out on the same night. He had decided to give up if she said no. That night, Carol had tickets, which she had bought six months in advance, to see the movie *Exodus* that night with a friend. She asked her mother if she wanted to go in her place.

Abba took Carol to see a foreign film, but he didn't know the area and the movie theater was not on the street where he had expected to find it. Carol, who had grown up in the city, knew exactly where the theater was. It was a terrible Russian film and everyone was smoking, but it was a successful first date. They went to the photo booth and took a picture together, which currently sits in a picture frame on Abba's desk. They're looking at each other and laughing. I have seen that picture my whole life and thought they were already married when it was taken.

After that, Abba used to meet her after school. All the girls were jealous that Carol had a college guy waiting. On their second date, Abba told Carol he was going to marry her.

He was right. The wedding was on a Sunday afternoon in a New York wedding hall in 1963. When Abba stomped on the glass,[1] he pretended to hurt his foot. When it was time to kiss the bride, he turned

---

[1] In Jewish weddings, it is customary for the groom to crush a glass underneath his foot to commemorate the destruction of the temple. It's a slight damper on an otherwise joyous event, but that's Jewish tradition for you.

Culture Shock

around and kissed his mother instead. They took their honeymoon in Puerto Rico.

In 1966, they went on a six-month program to Israel sponsored by the Committee on Man Power Opportunities in Israel. They fell in love with the country and decided to move there. The program guaranteed a job, but there were none available, so it paid for their return to the States. They moved to Manhattan, Kansas to get their graduate degrees, deciding to return to Israel when they could both find jobs. My father, Avi, and my aunt, Rachel, were born in Kansas.

Kansas State University's grain science programs attracted kibbutzniks[2] from kibbutzim around Israel. The Rubins became close with an Israeli woman who babysat Avi and Rachel and was a leader in the kibbutz movement. She convinced them to live in a kibbutz in Kfar HaMaccabi, which produced grain in the north of Haifa. She arranged for their travel and residence in the kibbutz. The Rubins decided to try it. Carol had job offers in the Ben-Gurion University of the Negev, Tel Aviv University, and the Technion— Israel Institute of Technology in Haifa. They had always wanted to live in Haifa. Carol took a position as a professor of mechanical engineering at the Technion.

---

[2] People who live in kibbutzim, communal villages founded by immigrant youth movements. The Macabbi Youth Movement from Germany and Russia established Kfar HaMaccabi in 1936. It was the largest producer of animal feed in Israel.

There were no positions for Abba, but they decided to move anyway. In 1971, when Avi was three, and their daughter Tova only a year old, they made Aliyah[3] to Israel.

In the kibbutz system, couples worked on the kibbutz in rotating duties: sometimes in the dining room, in the laundry, the fields, the children's house, other times in the orchard. As a rare exception, one spouse could work outside the kibbutz. In most kibbutzim, children spent the day and slept in the children's house, but in Kfar HaMaccabi, they slept with their parents. In an experiment for the kibbutz movement, Abba and Carol both had outside jobs. At this point, Abba had talked his way into getting a job as a professor of English literature at Haifa University. Their salaries went to the kibbutz.

Carol appreciated the thought that she would never have to cook again, but she soon noticed that many people didn't eat in the dining room. They took food back to their houses. Privacy and quiet were rare on the kibbutz. Families put their laundry outside their doors, to be done by whoever was assigned to laundry in that rotation. There were different days for sheets, for darks, and for lights. Carol didn't understand Hebrew well and could not follow the schedule. The laundry piled up in their home, so she took out new bedding to use. One day, a woman from the laundry

---

[3] Literally means "going up"; the migration of Jews to Israel from the diaspora

called out across the kibbutz, "Don't you ever change your linen?"

On Shabbat, children above a certain age were allowed to spend the day with their parents. Younger children stayed in the children's home. Avi was old enough to stay with his parents, but Rachel was not. She didn't want to stay in the children's house, so her parents let her stay with them. The kibbutz leaders came into the dining hall and asked why Rachel wasn't in the children's house. All the kids her age had to go.

When a woman wanted shoes, someone would take her size, go into town and pick out a pair of shoes. The woman could not pick the shoes herself. Individuality was not something that was celebrated. If someone wished to engage in an activity, the kibbutz voted on it, and if it was approved, paid for it. Nobody made decisions for themselves. The kibbutz gave members everything they needed, but they had no possessions of their own.

Abba and Carol were too independent for this sort of lifestyle. After three and a half months, they moved to Haifa and rented a two-bedroom apartment. The windows were not well sealed, and the wind blew loudly through the building and their room. After a year, their lease was ending, and the landlord was selling the apartment. The Rubins did not have enough money to buy, and it was hard to find rental space in Israel. The Jewish Agency was offering apartments, but the new buildings were already full of *olim hadashim*, or new immigrants. Abba and Carol were put on a waiting list.

One morning, they received a call from an American friend, who was leasing an apartment in an unfinished building. He told them that one family was giving up their apartment in that building, and Abba and Carol were next on the waiting list. A large apartment for Israel, it was considered luxurious. Carol called their agent at the Jewish Agency and inquired about the new apartment.

"Well, I don't know," the agent replied. Carol called Abba, who told her that they should give up. Carol went downtown to the agency and learned that the family was moving to Beersheva and had requested the apartment be given to their friends, another American family. Like Carol, the husband had a PhD in engineering, and he also worked for the ministry of defense. The Rubins had three children, and the other family had only one child. They claimed that the wife was in her first trimester of pregnancy, but she had no doctor's letter or any other kind of evidence.[4]

Carol went to her agent's office and explained that her family deserved the apartment. The Rubin family was next on the waiting list. He knew what was right, and he knew what was fair.

"I'm sitting down here until I get the apartment," she said. The agent was going crazy. He

---

[4] They found out later that she didn't have a baby. At this point in the interview, Bubbe responded, "They had real hutzpah!"

Culture Shock

had meetings, he had work, and he didn't have time for this. The apartment went to my grandparents.[5]

When moving day arrived, the ten-story building had no elevators, the grounds weren't cleared, and there was no clearance issued that it was safe. There was also no date assuring people when they could move in.

The residents who already knew each other decided to march on Amidar, the public housing company, and demand the keys to their apartments. Above the uproar of angry immigrants, Amidar claimed that the apartments weren't safe. The families said that they didn't care, that they were going to move in. They agreed to sign a waiver, but the agency said that would be impossible. One angry man from Boston banged his first on the table and called the clerk a bastard in Hebrew. The clerk was horribly offended, and everyone began yelling in different languages in different accents.

"It's my lunchtime," the clerk shouted, proceeding to take out a bag and eat his sandwich. The room became quiet.

"Bete'avon!"[6] one woman called out.

Finally, the families were promised their keys and an upcoming move-in date.

At this meeting, my grandparents met their lifelong friends, the Cohens, after discovering that

---

[5] At this point, Bubbe blushed and claimed that she wasn't a terribly assertive person.
[6] Hebrew for "bon appetite"

their second-floor apartment was directly above the Cohens'. Although their apartment was worth more, my grandparents offered to switch to the first floor, so they wouldn't have to worry about their young children bothering the neighbors. The Cohens refused.

My father and his siblings grew up in a variety of cultures and personalities. My grandparents' upstairs neighbors from Austria boasted beautiful paintings by students of Rembrandt. The apartment across from them belonged to a Russian family with twin boys and an older girl who babysat the children. Above them was another family with children my father's age. Every family moved into the building at the same time, and all the kids went to school together.

There was a family from Argentina. The parents were both psychologists and had unconventional ideas on disciplining their children. That is to say, Carol thought the children were monsters. They defecated on bridges where people walked. They banged on the Rubin's door until Carol opened it, and then they ran into the apartment, dragging crayons across the wall. One time, Rachel came home crying. "Ariel bit me," she said.

Carol was furious. She went upstairs, caught the kid, and dragged him to his father. "Take a look at what your son just did to my daughter."

The father looked disappointed and turned to his son. "Lama Arielito? Lama?" Why Arielito, Why? Like biting Rachel was just a cute thing his son had done.

Culture Shock

There was a press photographer from Romania who moved to Israel with his family. The government put him up with a helicopter. In Israel, he owned and operated a photography business. He was opening another store with his business partner, a Russian photographer, and wanted a loan from the government. At the Jewish Agency, they filled out paperwork, waited through long lines, and accumulated document upon document. They traveled to Tel Aviv again and again and went through the same process.

"I tell you what," the Russian partner said. "You keep your money." He flipped a desk over, and the agent ran out of the way. But he got his loan.

My uncle Yaacov was born four months before the Yom Kippur War. In the months preceding the war, there had already been several false alarms. A week before fighting broke out, Egypt began moving forces into the Suez Canal zone, but Israeli military intelligence believed this to be a military exercise. At the time, there was an optimistic feeling in Israel. After the Six-Day War in 1967, in which Israel won the Sinai, the Gaza Strip, the West Bank, East Jerusalem, and the Golan Heights, the country became overconfident, which fed into its sense of invulnerability.

Golda Meir was the first female prime minister of Israel, and she too was confident that the Arab nations would eventually recognize Israel. When President Anwar el-Sadat of Egypt made a peace proposal that involved Israel withdrawing from the Suez Canal and all territory captured in the Six-Day War, Meir would not concede until Egypt agreed to border changes and recognition of Israel.

Egypt's economy could not handle its campaign against Israel. Knowing that peace plans would not be in his favor, Sadat cut ties with his Soviet advisers and began diplomatic relations with government officials in Washington DC, who would be needed in future peace talks. Meanwhile, Egypt and Syria formed an alliance and planned a secret attack.

Once they realized they were under attack, Israeli officials wanted to call a preemptive strike, but the Defense Minister and Meir decided against it. Mossad[7] spies reported that war was coming, but military intelligence dismissed the warning. On the holiest day of the year, many soldiers were observing Yom Kippur and were not stationed at their posts.

On October 6, 1973, Abba left early for synagogue. An hour or so later, Carol left with the children and heard planes. She met up with a friend, who said that she saw them streaking across the sky, coming from over the Golan. They would have to wait until after sundown, when Shabbat was over, to find out what happened. Carol laughed that she would call their friends from the Golan for good news. They went to synagogue.

---

[7] HaMossad leModi'in ule Tafkidim Meyuhadim (Institute for Intelligence and Special Operations), the national intelligence agency of Israel

Culture Shock

They returned home at one in the afternoon, and as they were entering their apartment building, sirens went off. They had never heard the sirens before. Nobody was downstairs yet, so they were the first ones to descend to the shelter. It filled up with immigrants, people who hadn't heard sirens since World War II, who came to Israel expecting to find a better life. People were crying hysterically, including the nanny who cared for baby Yaacov. She was originally from Egypt and her grandson was on the battlefront, and she made herself sick thinking about him. She handed the baby back to Carol. The radio was turned on, and they found out that Egypt had attacked the Sinai, and Syria had attacked the Golan, catching the IDF by surprise.

One of Carol and Abba's colleagues, a mechanical engineer on reserve duty in the Golan, was killed on the first day of fighting. The colleague who helped Carol and Abba get their apartment was also on the battlefront, driving a yellow Volvo station wagon. When he drove back to Haifa, his car looked like Swiss cheese, but he survived.

The war went on. At night, they covered the windows in a black out. When sirens sounded at midnight, they went downstairs to the bomb shelter, taking Yaacov in his carriage, where he was sleeping. People were annoyed that they had to take the stairs. They didn't like being slowed down.

When he arrived in Israel, Abba had volunteered to join the Israeli Defense Force. They interviewed him, found out about his messed up eye, that he didn't know how to shoot, and that he had no experience with the armed services, and told him, "Forget it. Go home. You want to help the Israeli army? Join the Egyptian army."

When the war came, Abba was not summoned, but he had to help. He jumped into his car. All the roads were empty. He zoomed down to Hadar HaCarmel and found the volunteer center. A man told him to go downstairs to a girl who would take his information. Abba ran down the stairs, three or four steps at a time.

The girl asked him if he had a car. He said yes. She asked for his name and telephone number. "We'll call you."

After a few days, Abba realized they weren't going to call him. He found another center and volunteered his car. He was assigned to pick up a group of Georgian Jews from Haifa. In the middle of a caravan of a hundred cars, he lost sight of the car in front of him at a crossroad. The cars behind him were waiting. Abba sat for a few seconds and guessed. By chance, or maybe Rubin luck, he caught up with the rest of the group and arrived where his passengers were waiting. Abba's car was a seven-passenger car, but these men were massive. When they got into the car, it sank to the ground. Abba never went out of second gear. He had to put the car in first gear just to get it to move. But he made it to their destination, from Karmiel to Haifa.

Culture Shock

Iraq joined the fight against Israel on the third day of fighting, and Syria soon received support from Jordan. President Nixon delayed a U.S. airlift of arms to Israel to show sympathy for Egypt. Low on equipment and men, Israel began its defense against the Arab coalition. Meir refused to deploy Israel's nuclear arsenal bombs, and instead, enlisted help from the United States. President Nixon airlifted aircrafts, tanks, and arms to Israel. With this support, Israel pushed back and recaptured the Golan. A cease-fire began on October 25th.

After the war, in 1974, when he was thirty-three years old, Abba received a notice from the army to report downtown. When he arrived, the doors were still locked, and there were only three people waiting to enter the building. As time passed, a mass formed, and the doors opened to a madhouse. Somehow, the door got locked again, and Abba had to call someone through the window to open it. The officers took Abba to get equipment. They handed him a gun.

"Teach me how to use it, then I'll take it. But until then, no thanks," Abba said. They let him by and told him to go to the parade grounds, where a man was calling out names. It was a large area, but covered completely by the crowd. As the man called out names into groups, a sergeant led them away. Abba was left standing there after everyone had gone. He approached the man with the names and said that he had not been called. The man told him to report back at eight o'clock the next morning.

At eight o'clock sharp, he was one of eight men in the building. He was surrounded by crazy looking people, and he knew he was in trouble. An officer arrived and started writing down information. Abba repeated that he had no experience in the army. He was exempt from the American army draft because of his eye. He had a PhD.

"In what?" the officer asked.

"English literature."

"Great," the officer said. He gathered a group of men together. "This is what I want you to do. Take a pad of paper and walk around the base and write down anything you see that can be improved, as long as it doesn't cost money."

Abba walked around and wrote poems on his pad. He asked when he could go home.

"According to your conscience," the man said. Abba slept at home and came to the base every day. After three days of wandering the grounds, another officer approached him and told him he had an assignment for him.

His new boss was a troubled eighteen-year-old jock who couldn't call him "Abba"[8] because he had a bad relationship with his father. Abba met him in a parking lot where a truck was being unloaded. When the truck started pulling out, the boy ran and jumped onto the cargo bed. Abba followed him. He sat down

---

[8] Besides being my zayde's name, Abba is also the Hebrew word for father

Culture Shock

but decided to stand instead so he wouldn't break his spine. He worked with this kid for about five days, performing odd jobs, schlepping[9] various objects. He was then assigned to a disabled man, who worked in a shed, moving missiles and bombs around. The man had trouble with his legs and wasn't able to carry the munitions, so he told Abba where they were supposed to be relocated. Abba picked up the weapons, which were heavy, like stones, but he was not about to drop them. He did this for about a week, after which he completed his army duty.

In the aftermath of the war, Israel lost artillery, aircrafts, money, and its sense of invincibility. Golda Meir stepped down as prime minister. As an offer of peace, Israel returned the Sinai to Egypt and signed the first peace agreement between Israel and an Arab nation. Syria was left in total defeat, and along with other Arab nations, voted to expel Egypt from the Arab League.

Israel's universities were state government-funded universities, and all eight institutes ceased hiring. They also stopped giving tenure, and as a result, Abba and Carol were fired. They had no choice but to move back to America. There was an opening in engineering at the University of Birmingham, Alabama. The chairman of the department was in Israel for a conference and interviewed Carol for the

---

[9] Yiddish for carrying something, usually awkwardly or with difficulty

position. Abba called up the chairman of the English department, who was Jewish.

In the summer of 1976, they packed and schlepped seventeen boxes back to New York. It was a big financial decision to take two taxis, but they had no choice. Abba took all the boxes in one taxi and Carol took the children in another. One of them ended up at the wrong hotel. Abba spent the entire evening moving boxes, trying to find the family. In the end, they were reunited.

Although they were from the North and knew "that in the South people owned other people and alligators roamed the streets,"[10] both got jobs in Birmingham and settled back down in America, without looking back at the homeland they were leaving behind.

---

[10] In Zayde's words

The Invention of the Wheel

I.

Once upon a time, a long long time ago, there was a drought. People prayed to God, offered sacrifices, but no rain fell to quench their thirst and water their crops. One scholar named Honi took a stick and drew a circle around himself in the mud.

"I'm not leaving until there is rain," he said. It began to drizzle. Honi declared that he wasn't satisfied. So it began to pour. Then Honi explained that he wanted a gentle, calm rain. The rain slowed to a decent rate.

Once he left the circle, Honi was threatened with excommunication for showing dishonor toward God. He was excused by Prince Shimon ben Shetach because Honi had a special relationship with God.

It is interesting that Honi chose a circle, a shape symbolizing wholeness and infiniteness. Circles appear in nature as the cycle of life, in patterns of tree trunks, and sinking whirlpools. But man-made circles have spun just as long. Take the wheel for example, invented in 3500 BC in Mesopotamia. No wheels exist in nature. They're an entirely human invention. In the Bronze Age, the wheel was used for pottery to create pots and pans, as humans planted crops and tended to their animals. Scholars believe the wheel soon spread to other places in the world, or it was developed in other locations independently.

Newton's first law of motion states that an object in motion continues in motion with the same speed and in the same direction unless acted upon by an unbalanced force. As a wheel begins rolling down a hill, it begins slowly and moves faster and faster.

In the 15th century, Leonardo da Vinci created models and designs for transportation vehicles, a clockwork car powered by springs. In 1769, Nicolas Joseph Cugnot designed a three wheeled steam-engineered tractor, known as the first car. It was heavy and difficult to steer. He had the first ever car crash when he hit a brick wall. He was charged with speeding and thrown in jail. In 1885, Karl Benz created the first gas-powered car. Henry Ford launched the Model T in 1908. Fifteen million were sold, garnering over a billion dollars.

Suddenly, the wheel became essential. The world is different now, congested with highways and traffic signs. It's impossible to get anywhere without a car. We are so used to the wheel, we can't live without it, and we don't know when the dependency began. Like all things that spin in circles, it requires closer examination.

II.

Sibling rivalries are as old as siblings themselves. Cain couldn't think clearly. He stood in the Arabian desert, facing the wind, his brother's blood on his hands. He had committed the first murder. The wind knocking against him seemed to carry his brother's screams. This feeling was guilt, but he did not know it. So he fought it. He refused responsibility. He took his curse and bore it. Maybe that would take away the pain, but it stayed with him, like his mark. Cain wandered the desert. Nobody could look at him. He was untouchable.

III

In 1987, an Israeli was stabbed to death while shopping in Gaza. A day later, an Israeli truck crashed into a station wagon, killing four Palestinians. Believing the crash to be intentional retaliation, Palestinians rioted, taking to the street with rocks, burning tires, and Molotov cocktails. A seventeen-year-old was killed by an Israeli soldier after throwing a Molotov cocktail at an Israel patrol car, and violence spread throughout the West Bank. This event became known as the First Intifada. During this event, Sheikh Ahmed Yassin, an activist in the Muslim Brotherhood who preached and performed charity work in the West Bank and Gaza Strip, established Hamas, the Islamic Resistance Movement.

In 1988, Yassir Arafat, the leader of the PLO, agreed to recognize Israel's right to exist and make peace, with the establishment of a self-governed entity in a small part of Palestine. Israel agreed to recognize the PLO and evacuate most of the West Bank and Gaza Strip. The same year, Hamas published its charter, which called for the destruction of Israel and the establishment of an Islamic society in Palestine instead.

In 1992, Yitzhak Rabin became Prime Minister and halted settlements in occupied territory. In April of 1993, a member of Hamas blew up his car beside a parked Israeli bus in the Jordan Valley. Two passengers were killed and five wounded. This was the first of Hamas' suicide bombing attacks on Israel, a tactic for which they would eventually become known. Between the first bombing and the Second Intifada in 2000, 37 suicide bombs exploded in Israel.

In September, Foreign Minister of Israel, Shimon Peres, and PLO representative Mahmoud Abbas met in Washington D.C. to sign The Oslo Peace Accord, or the Declaration of Principles on Interim Self-Government Arrangements, in which Israel agreed to withdraw troops from the Gaza Strip and the city of Jericho in the West Bank, remaining in control of the borders between the autonomous and outside areas and the Jewish settlements. The accord called for a Palestinian government that would exercise authority over the West Bank.

I.

In 3200 BCE, the wheel was first used for transportation purposes as Mesopotamian chariots. In 2000 BCE, Egyptians invented the spoked wheel, which came in handy when the wheelbarrow was invented in ancient Greece, around 408 BCE. The wheelbarrow spread around the world, increasing labor and bringing more earnings. Four centuries later, it showed up in China and spread to medieval Europe through Byzantium and the Islamic world.

In North America, wheels were not used for transportation, but as playthings for children, including netted hoops and animals on wheels. When Columbus arrived, the wheel was introduced into indigenous life as a tool, along with disease and slavery. Wooden hoops were left in the dirt as tribes were pushed off their land. Exile and trails of tears: these too are things of wheels.

II.

Sarai could not bear a child, and she knew this hurt her husband, who had been promised descendants as numerous as the stars. She offered her handmaid, Hagar, to Abram. Hagar gave birth to Ishmael, causing Sarai to grow spiteful and jealous. Eventually, she chased Hagar out of the house, leaving Hagar and Ishmael lost, wandering the desert. They ran out of food and water. Hagar held the boy in her arms and sat and cried. Suddenly, she was called in the night. An angel told her that God knew her child was suffering. Ishmael would become the father of a mighty nation and she should return to Sarai's home.

Ishmael grew up to be a leader, a fierce warrior as God promised, with twelve sons. Meanwhile, Abraham brought his son up a mountain and instructed him to build an altar. His son asked where they would find a lamb for the sacrifice. Abraham, with a tight throat, told him not to worry about it.

Abraham tied his son to the altar and brought down his knife. An angel caught his arm and told him that he had obeyed God's command and did not need to sacrifice his son. Instead, he found a ram to sacrifice. They went home, the boy breathing heavily, stiff at his father's grip on his shoulder. In the Torah, the boy is Isaac. In the Koran, it is Ishmael.

III

In 1968, Rabbi Meir Kuhane founded the Jewish Defense, a radical organization designed to protect Jews by "whatever means possible," advocating violence and anti-Muslim sentiment to combat anti-Semitism. In February of 1994, a member of the Jewish Defense League, Baruch Goldstein, an American physician who had immigrated to Israel, walked into the Ibrahim Mosque at the Cave of the Patriarchs in Hebron, fully armed, and opened fire on worshipping Palestinians. Before being beaten to death by survivors, he killed 29 Palestinians and wounded 125.

Riots broke out across the West Bank, leading to the death of 26 more Palestinians and nine Israelis. Angry mobs tried to attack worshippers at the Western Wall and Palestinian youths chucked rocks at policemen stationed below the Temple Mount. Police responded with rubber bullets and tear gas. Demanding vengeance, Hamas orchestrated two attacks against Israeli civilians. Prime Minister Yitzhak Rabin and the United Nations Security Council condemned the attacks, calling on Israel to guarantee the safety of Palestinians. President of Israel Ezer

Weizman called the killings "the worst thing that has happened to us in the history of Zionism."

In May of 1994, Israel completed its withdrawal from the Gaza Strip and Jericho. Arafat established the Palestinian Authority in Jericho as his government. Israel also signed a peace treaty with Jordan. Arafat, Rabin, and Shimon Peres won the Nobel Peace Prize for their efforts.

In 1995, Rabin and Arafat signed the Oslo II Accords. Israeli forces agreed to withdraw from the West Bank's six largest cities. Three percent of the territories in the West Bank, which held one third of the Palestinian population, fell under the command of the Palestinian Authority. The West Bank was divided into three sections: one with exclusive Palestinian control, one with Israeli control, and one with Palestinian civilian control and Israeli security control. In the Gaza Strip, Israel retained 35 percent of the land, containing Jewish settlements, and gave the rest to the leadership of the Palestinian Authority.

At a peace rally in Tel Aviv, Prime Minister Rabin was assassinated by an Israeli law student who supported the Israeli settlers. After president Anwar el-Sadat, Rabin was the second Middle Eastern leader to be killed by extremists on his own side. Shimon Peres became the next Prime Minister, but peace was stalled under his leadership and that of the next two prime ministers, Benjamin Netanyahu and Ehud Barak.

Elana Rubin

In 2000, President Clinton invited Prime Minister Barak and Arafat to Camp David to negotiate the Israeli-Palestinian conflict, but the summit ended without an agreement. Ariel Sharon, the leader of the right-winged Likud party, visited the Temple Mount, a Muslim controlled religious location for both Jews and Muslims, with a large police presence, leading to a new wave of violence: the Second Intifada. Palestinian youths threw rocks at Israeli soldiers. Armed Israeli police hurled tear gas, fire, and rubber coated bullets, backed by tanks and Blackhawk helicopter gunships. In Gaza, a twelve-year-old Palestinian boy was caught in crossfire and killed. In Ramallah, two Israeli reservists were killed at a Palestinian police outpost; one was thrown out a window and trampled by a crowd. In retaliation, Israel sent rockets and bombs on Palestinian offices and targets in Gaza and the West Bank. Suicide bombing attacks increased more frequently in Israel. Since the Second Intifada began, 164 bombs detonated in Israel, and 450 terrorists were arrested before they could commit a bombing. Attacks occurred most commonly in shopping malls, buses, street corners, and largely congregated areas. Between October of 2000 and April of 2006, around 300 Israelis were killed from suicide attacks. In that period, almost 5,000 people, mostly Palestinians, were killed.

I.

In the Middle Ages, punishments included being stretched across a wheel and beaten to death, or having an iron wheel bound across the bones with a

Culture Shock

hammer. In the early fourth century, Saint Catherine of Alexandria was rolled across the ground, wrapped around the rim of a spiked wheel. According to legend, the wheel broke, and she lived until the Romans beheaded her. The breaking wheel became known as the "Catherine Wheel."

II.

Of Isaac's two sons, Esau was the tough brother, the hunter, whose claim to the birthright made him the heir and successor of his father. Jacob, the quiet, studious one, bought the birthright from his brother in exchange for a bowl of stew. Jacob went to Isaac's tent, wearing sheepskin, disguised as Esau's burly arms. Isaac had lost his vision and granted Jacob the blessing. When Esau heard that Jacob had the birthright, he vowed to kill his brother. Jacob fled.

Twenty years later, after Jacob had settled down with his wives Rachel and Leah, he met his brother again. Expecting a battle, Jacob advised his men to prepare. But his brother ran and embraced him, kissed him. They wept together.

III.

In 2002, Israel seized the *Karine A*, a ship carrying 50 tons of rockets, mines, antitank missiles, and other weapons to the Palestinian Authority. The Bush administration's envoy, Anthony Zinni, had recently met with Arafat to strengthen the cease-fire with Israel. Arafat denied any connection to the ship and claimed that Israel fabricated the story as propaganda against the Palestinian Authority and to undermine the cease-fire efforts of the United States.

In March, a Palestinian terrorist detonated himself in a hotel in Netanya, where a Passover seder was taking place with 250 people. Hamas claimed responsibility, and the attack was praised in Palestinian media. From September 2000 to February 2002, almost 300 Israelis were killed by Palestinian terrorists.

The day after the attack, in response to a UN Security Council resolution calling for a two state solution of a Palestinian State side by side with Israel, the Arab League drafted the Saudi Plan, the first Pan-Arab peace initiative in the Middle East. In the plan, the Arab countries hoped to have the same relationship with Israel as any other state, offering normal relations in return for Israeli withdrawal from occupied Arab territories, the creation of an independent Palestinian state with al-Quds al-Shareef, or East Jerusalem as the capital, and the return of refugees. The United States discouraged Israel from pursuing peace with Syria because of its alliance with Iran. Along with the recent Hamas attack, Israel rejected the plan.

Two days after the attack, the IDF began Operation Defensive Shield, a military offensive into six of the largest cities in the West Bank and surrounding towns, villages, and refugee camps to root out Palestinian terrorists. The Operation, involving Israeli troops and vehicles entering cities, imposing curfews, arresting Palestinians who were believed to be involved in armed actions against Israel, and destroying infrastructure believed to be operated by militant groups, ended on April 21. More than 6,000 Palestinians were arrested during Operation Defensive Shield. The IDF's incursion into Area A, which was controlled exclusively by the Palestinian Authority, resulted in 497 Palestinian deaths. In early April, Palestinians claimed that Israeli-Palestinian fighting in the Jenin refugee camp was a massacre of Palestinian civilians. The UN rejected this report.

In July, Israel bombed the home of Sheikh Salah Shehadeh, the military leader of Hamas, burying him with at least 11 other Palestinians and wounding 120. In 2003, Arafat elevated Mahmud Abbas to Prime Minister of the Palestinian Authority. With Abbas' commitment to decrease attacks on Israeli civilians, the United States released a plan for peace in the Middle East with the creation of a Palestinian state by 2005.

In June, Israel began constructing a West Bank security wall to prevent suicide bombers and terrorists from crossing into populated Israeli centers. The European Union formally condemned the building of the wall. With anti-Semitism present in Europe, Israeli foreign minister Silvan Shalom demanded a more balanced EU stance in the conflict, ensuring that the fence would be dismantled with a peace settlement. While recognizing Israel's right to protect itself, the EU said that the fence could prevent the creation of a

Palestinian state and urged Israel to avoid civilian causalities and end extra-judicial killings. The World Court ruled that the West Bank wall violated international law and urged Israel to tear it down and compensate Palestinians harmed by the construction. In 2004, Israeli Prime Minister Ariel Sharon announced that he would dismantle Israeli settlements in the Gaza Strip, including the withdrawal of 7,500 Israelis who lived in the settlements.

In 2004, Hamas also increased Qassam rocket attacks. In a rocket attack on Sderot, a city in the western Negev, on June 28, two Israelis were killed, including a four-year-old when a Qassam landed in his nursery school. In September two more Israeli children were killed in Sderot from another rocket attack that hit their apartment buildings. In response, the IDF launched a three-week operation, in which 130 Palestinians, including 68 Hamas and Islamic Jihad militants, and five Israelis died.

In November of 2005, Yassir Arafat died and Mahmoud Abbas, the leader of the Fatah party, was elected president of the Palestinian Authority. Hamas and Islamic Jihad agreed to suspend attacks on Israel so that Abbas could guarantee a ceasefire to end more than four years of intifada. Abbas told Palestinian television that it was essential for Israel to end the targeting of armed Islamist groups. Israel removed the last Jewish settlers and protesters from the Gaza strip and moved to the final stages of withdrawal.

I.

Culture Shock

In 1791, a year after the US Patent Law was passed, James Macomb received the first patent involving a wheel: the water wheel to create hydropower for mills. The original record was destroyed in a fire in 1836. In 2001, in Australia, John Keogh, a patent lawyer, submitted a patent for a "circular transportation facilitation device." He was trying to prove that the new patent system, allowing inventors to draft patents online without the help of a lawyer, was flawed. He was issued the patent, and the wheel was reinvented.

II.

I was a jealous older sibling. My brother learned to ride a bike before I could. I was seven and he was just three years old. My face fell as he was congratulated. I threw my bike down and stormed back into my house. Growing up with twin siblings was difficult. They shared a strong bond I had never been a part of. They liked to pretend they were telepathic. In Israel, I was in charge of babysitting them while my parents went out to dinner. They told me they were born with the sole purpose of annoying me. They plotted against me and fought with me and teased me. I fought back, but it was two of them against one. When my parents arrived, we were reading in our respective rooms, fuming.

We argue over word choices and whether we are entitled to our stupid opinions. We have been doing so since we were young children, and I imagine it will continue throughout adulthood. I don't like the person I am when I fight with my siblings. I am incapable of raising my voice at anyone else. I am too mature to be fighting over seating and the equal division of a bag of candy.

I swear I won't keep in touch with my siblings when we are adults. My parents try to convince me otherwise. They tell me, "Friends will come and go, but you will always have family."

III.

In 2006, Hamas won a majority of the Palestinian parliamentary election, with Abbas, the leader of Fatah, still the president of the Palestinian Authority. This would complicate matters of peace under the U.S.-initiated "road map," which proposed a two-state solution, while Hamas believed that Israel should be replaced by a Palestinian state. In Israel, Kadima, a centrist party dedicated to withdrawing from the West Bank, won the parliamentary election. On July 12th, Hezbollah, a militia Shiite group in Lebanon, fired a pair of rockets into northern Israel. Guerilla fighters captured two Israeli soldiers during an attack along the Lebanese border between the Israeli towns of Zar'it and Shtula. Eight Israeli soldiers died fighting. In response, Israeli ground, air, and naval forces attacked eight Hezbollah bases and five bridges in southern Lebanon. During the 34 days of the Israel-Lebanon War, 4,000 rockets were fired into northern Israel. A ceasefire was called on August 14th. More than 908 Lebanese and 159 Israelis were killed during the war.

Fatah initially refused to join Hamas in a grand coalition, and each party built up its own security forces. Following negotiations brokered by Saudi Arabia, Fatah and Hamas entered a Palestinian national unity government on March 7, 2007. After a week of factional fighting between Hamas and Fatah in June caused the death of more than 100 people, Hamas militants seized the presidential compound in Gaza City. Abbas dissolved the unity government of Hamas and Fatah and declared a state of emergency. Hamas continued to govern the Gaza Strip, limiting the authority of the Palestinian national Authority under Abbas to the West Bank.

Israel and Egypt ordered a blockade of all cargo shipments to the Gaza Strip, putting tighter restrictions on borders. It became difficult for Palestinians to leave Gaza and obtain building materials and food. Israel was criticized harshly by human rights organizations.

In November, as revenge against Israel's closing of Gaza crossings, Hamas fired rockets into Israel, sending 18 Israelis to the hospital. Israeli military officials discovered and destroyed a tunnel dug by Hamas militants on the Israeli-Gaza border. Knowing that attempting to wipe out Hamas would require an invasion of all of Gaza and reoccupation, the Israeli army moved into Gaza to prevent Hamas from firing rockets and to pressure them into accepting a cease-fire. Despite this, Hamas continued to send rockets into Israel. After destruction and 1,300

Palestinian deaths and thirteen Israeli deaths, Israel announced a ceasefire, and troops left Gaza. In 2009, Benjamin Netanyahu of the right-winged Likud party became Prime Minister. United States President Barack Obama demonstrated his support for a two-state solution and called on Israel to stop settlements in the West Bank. Netanyahu endorsed a Palestinian state, with conditions such as having no army and recognizing Israel as the Jewish state. The Palestinians rejected the offer.

In 2010, Israel commandos boarded a flotilla of ships carrying aid for Gaza. This was the ninth attempt since 2008 to break the Israeli and Egyptian blockade of the Gaza Strip. Descending on ropes from helicopters, they landed on the largest ship and were attacked by the activists on board, who claimed the commandos began shooting as soon as they landed. Israeli officials claimed they fired in self-defense. Nine activists died and thirty people were wounded.

In January 2011, leaked documents revealed that Abbas was willing to make concessions for peace, including that it was illogical to ask Israel to take in five million refugees. In March, Hamas fired more than 50 rockets into Israel. In May, Fatah and Hamas signed a reconciliation pact, with the formation of an interim government over the West Bank and the Gaza Strip. President Obama called for peace negotiations to begin, with the borders from before the 1967 Six-Day War. He asked for the carrying out of a full withdrawal of Israeli military force from the West Bank, with a future Palestinian state without a military, to be created.

In September, Abbas sought full membership for a Palestinian state in the United Nations, which the United States threatened to veto. The U.S. wanted to achieve a Palestinian state through Israel-Palestinian agreements and not the United Nations. Palestine became the 195th member of UNESCO. After failing to come to a unanimous decision on Palestinian statehood, in 2012, the United Nations votes to accept Palestine as a non-member observer state. With no progress for peace between Israel and Jordan, and continued rocket attacks by Hamas against Israel from Gaza, flowed by Israeli defense operations against Hamas militants, Netanyahu claimed that he wanted a peaceful two state solution, but he did not believe it was realistically possible. "For that, circumstances have to change."

In 2015, the Vatican recognized the state of Palestine. Violence between Israelis and Palestinians escalated. Israeli Defense Minister Moshe Ya'alon signed a decree banning Murabitun and Murabatat Islamist activist groups, which gathered on the Temple Mount to intimidate and shout at Jewish visitors. Abbas stated that the Jews "[had] no right to desecrate [Al-Aqsa and the Church of the Holy Sepulcher] with their filthy feet." In the West Bank and Gaza border, Palestinians burned tires and threw rocks as Israeli forces responded with tear gas, rubber bullets, and live ammunition.

Violence continues with the latest trend: Palestinian teens stabbing Israelis without political or organizational support. The death rates rise on both sides, and nothing has changed since the creation of Israel.

IV.

When I was in second grade, three IDF soldiers were attacked in a cross border raid near Gaza. Palestinian militants crossed into Israel through an underground tunnel, and once on the Israeli side, sprayed fire and threw grenades toward their tank. The soldiers were Pavel Slutsker, Chanan Barak, and Gilad Shalit. In school, they began selling dog tags with the soldier's names on them for two dollars to donate to their families. I held mine in my hands and sang a prayer we had learned in school, "Veshavu banim lig'vulam, veyesh tikvah le'acharitech." And your children shall return to their own border, and there is hope for your future. Slutsker's and Barak's bodies were returned home in coffins. Gilad Shalit was still in captivity. There was hope.

Whenever there was an update on Gilad Shalit, my teachers set aside their lessons. We watched a video update that was recorded by Hamas. We talked about how it was probably fake, that they told him to say he was doing well. At camp every year on Israel Day, there was a station where we wrote messages to Gilad Shalit's family, who had set up a tent in Jerusalem. In seventh grade, when we were making art projects inspired by the story of Jonah and the whale,

Culture Shock

we heard news of the trade: in exchange for over a thousand Palestinian prisoners, Hamas released Gilad Shalit. That day, I came home and read every article I could on his return.

When I was younger, I tried to fix the world by donating my hair to girls with cancer. I asked for donations to an animal shelter instead of birthday gifts. I kept a jar marked "donations" dedicated to different causes, where I would leave my own money every once in a while. I dreamed that countries would disappear and everyone would care for one another because we were all human. I promised to always be naïve.

Eventually, I got used to the news and the abductions and the bombs and retaliations. I watched a video recently of a Palestinian telling Israeli soldiers to shoot his own child, so he could videotape it. Instead, the soldier shakes hands with the child. The father urges the child to throw rocks at the soldier. The child begins throwing rocks at the ground. I see videos of Palestinian teenagers celebrating the deaths of Israelis. I see a photo of a Palestinian store called "Hitler 2," featuring knife-wielding mannequins, to which the owner explains, "I like him because he was the most anti-Semitic person." I see Arabs holding up signs equating the Star of David with the Swastika.

From awe, to horror, to desensitization, violence on the television and newspaper became too much. I could only cry so many tears. I tried to distract myself to forget, spending hours each day watching shows until people in news footage blended with characters, until they were all just specks on the screen.

But the people on the news are real. I know that Palestinians feel trapped, surrounded by hate and poverty and fear. Even in the early days of Israel, Prime Minister Golda Meir said, "There will be peace when the Arabs love their own children more than they hate us." I know there are people who are scared of losing their jobs and their children going hungry. There are people who care so deeply for Palestinians that they turn their hate toward Israel. I see policy makers who only see the big picture and miss too many small details: individuals, families, and stories. I see people terrified of one another for being gay or Muslim or just different. I see people dying who don't deserve to die. I see people blaming each other and banning speakers from college campuses and I see loneliness.

I realize the history of the Palestinians and Israel is complicated. It has become so messy I can offer no solutions. At least not yet. Not until something changes. Bombings, retaliations, generations of hate repeat and will continue to repeat unless both sides want peace and are willing to have a discussion to attain it. We exist in a history dependent on the circular, repetitive motion of wheels. We have entangled ourselves in a twisted codependency of blame and death. We cannot fight hate with hate. That's already proven not to work.

Culture Shock

I am young, so it's natural for me to be hopeful. But I've also learned a lot in my seventeen years. I've learned that friendship is the most valuable gift life gives you, that perfection is boring and beauty is freedom, and that life ends and another generation goes on without us, growing from what we've left them. I've learned that kindness has become undervalued, when the one thing that pulled me out of the perfectionist, depressed hole I was digging, was kindness. I want overwhelming kindness. I want people to be vulnerable enough to understand that they don't know everything, to listen to each other, to help one another, to be real. I want people to see each other.

The same land intertwines our history. We are two nations begot by brothers. Jews and Muslims worship the same God. We are restricted from consuming pork by Kashrut and Halal. We abstain from food on Yom Kippur and Ramadan. Three times a day for Jews and five times a day for Muslims, we apportion time for prayer. Men and women are separated. Our recitations are chants of ancient melodies. Our languages are from the same Semitic origin. In Hebrew peace is "Shalom." In Arabic, it is "Salam."

Safety and Terrorism

When I was younger, I liked to collect pennies that I found on the ground and keep them in my pockets. Once when I was at camp, a Jewish camp, and I was bending down to pick up a penny, a girl called out, "You Jew!"

"It's for luck," I said but dropped the penny back on the ground anyway.

In my art camp the summer before fourth grade, I made up a counting song up to twenty-two, with an Elvis inspired tune and a disco inspired dance. Everyone dropped their clay and paint brushes to join in. I was pleased with myself for making so many friends. Three or four of the other children were Jewish, and we talked about how hard it was to keep Passover. A blonde girl sighed and made some sort of complaint ending with, "The *Jews* are talking."

After that, the Jews weren't talking. Lacking the courage to tell her that what she said made me uncomfortable, I stopped dancing and went back to my painting.

Culture Shock

The anti-Semitism I've experienced is minor, jokes gone too far. Most Jews are used to hearing them. When my mother was sixteen, she worked at Godfather's Pizza in Minnesota. Her co-workers made offensive comments about her Judaism and asked where her horns were. When my father was a student at the University of Michigan, his friend offered him a summer programming job in Howell, a small city in the north of Michigan. My dad used to go out for lunch by himself, and his friend suggested he not tell anyone he was Jewish because there was a large concentration of Klu Klux Klan.

"Won't they know by my name?" he said.

His friend told him, "No. They won't know that Avi Rubin is a Jewish or Israeli name. They don't know anything about Judaism."

In my Jewish History class at Krieger Schechter, we learned that anti-Semitism started from the beginning of history. After Jesus' crucifixion, the Romans destroyed the second temple in Jerusalem. The Jews were exiled and scattered all over the world. Christianity became the dominant religion in the Roman Empire. The Church condemned Jews for being agents of the devil, the murderers of Jesus. This last accusation was not renounced until Pope Benedict XVI absolved the Jews in 1960.

For many centuries in the Middle Ages, both state and church laws prevented Jews from owning land and holding public office. Meanwhile, guilds excluded Jews from many occupations, leaving them only with the options of money lending, tax collecting, or commerce. Thus began a stereotype that Jews are greedy. Excluded from society, Jews kept to themselves and their customs. Christians blamed Jews for poisoning wells and causing the Black Plague. Jews were drawn as devils with horns and cloven feet. Rumors such as the blood libel, in which Jews used the blood of Christian children in ritual sacrifices, were taken as truth. Both secular and religious states forced Jews into segregation, into districts called ghettos. Masses were expelled from England, France, Spain, Portugal, and German states. Jews began to migrate east.

With the Protestant Reformation, Martin Luther hoped tolerance would convince the Jews to convert. When the Jews refused, Luther instructed his followers to set synagogues on fire, to take away prayer books, and destroy houses, saying, "What does not burn must be covered over with earth so that no man will ever see stone or cinder of them again."

During the Enlightenment, European thinkers called for full rights to be returned to Jews on the condition they stop practicing their religion. Others blamed Judaism for perpetuating religious belief, which they believed to be illogical. Despite prejudice on secular, political, and social levels, many Jews were able to assimilate and become prominent citizens.

Still, violence against Jews was encouraged in the Russian Empire. Russian Jews were blamed for the assassination of Czar Alexander II in 1881, triggering pogroms in Kiev, Warsaw, and Odessa. Then in 1900, another rumor spread that Jews were conspiring to dominate the world using their money and intelligence to manipulate Christians. The Russian secret police forged a document supporting this assertion. "The Protocols of the Elders of Zion" was distributed worldwide, and still spreads today.

Pseudoscientific theories, mixed with well-established stereotypes about Jews, gained wide acceptance. The Jews were believed to be a separate race of Semites, with a different set of genetically inherited characteristics that made Jews dangerous and threatening. So by the time Hitler came around, anti-Semitism was widespread, and the Jews a convenient scapegoat for the horrors of WWI, the humiliation of Versailles, hyperinflation, and depression in Germany. Hitler believed Jews to be the root of all evils: disease, injustice, cultural decline, capitalism, and communism.

At the beginning of our Holocaust unit in eighth grade at Krieger Schechter, each student received a sketchbook and a plastic bag filled with art supplies, so we could record our complicated feelings throughout the year. When my teacher passed out copies of *Anne Frank: The Diary of a Young Girl,* I drew the cover, a picture of her, into my sketchbook. My teacher mentioned that she looked like me. We were the same age. She also wanted to be a writer. I imagined she was reading my thoughts just as I was reading hers. I dreaded finishing the book and reading the last entry:

> ...if I'm watched to that extent, I start by getting snappy, then unhappy, and finally I twist my heart round again, so that the bad is on the outside and the good is on the inside and keep on trying to find a way of becoming what I would so like to be, and I could be, if... there weren't any other people living in the world,
>
> Yours, Anne.

The next page was a historical note, and I got the eerie feeling that she had dropped off mid-conversation. I read how her father made it out of the war and found Anne's diaries. She was a better writer than me.

My class visited the Holocaust Museum in Washington D.C. I saw the shoe exhibit for the first time, hundreds of pairs piled up, spilled in different layers because they could not fit in one pile. I saw a picture of a boy whose collarbone and rib cage popped out of his skin. He was disintegrating. There are warning stickers over many of the exhibits: "Disturbing image." I accidently looked at a graphic image hidden behind a wall. Seeing the picture for only a second, I caught a sea of red and bony flesh stacked up so high it didn't look like bodies anymore. I almost puked in a cattle car because it smelled like death. I had never smelled death before, but I felt claustrophobic imagining hundreds of bodies stuffed in the tiny space, dropping on top of each other. Everything in that museum reeked of death. The objects and pictures of bodies were sad and made me too sick to eat or think about anything else, but they were still dead, from another world entirely. Maybe in a sick, twisted way, the Germans had succeeded. We did not see these people as humans. They were only dead bodies.

Then, I came to an exhibit with a high ceiling. At the top, faces of the Holocaust filled the walls. At the bottom, a deep pit filled with water reflected the faces. I met eyes with a girl who looked like me: dark hair, dark eyes, the slim Jewish nose. She could have been standing among my classmates at Krieger Schechter. Except she was in a picture frame, staring at the people who passed by, those of us who could leave the museum and put the Holocaust out of our minds.

In my sketchbook, I drew a crying eye with ominous scrawled letters spelling "Why?" Painting watercolor propaganda signs and sketching barbed wire fences did not help me sort out my feelings about the Holocaust. Still, dozens of poems and essays later, I cannot describe how I feel about it. I can't look at pictures of the gas chambers in Auschwitz, the piles of bodies, without crying. I'm overwhelmed. We lost six million and we don't understand why. The Holocaust is a big harsh word. Its presence cuts through and pushes everything else out of the way, so you're forced to look at it without an idea how to begin.

At the end of the year, my class visited the Israeli Holocaust museum Yad Vashem in Jerusalem. It contained most of the same artifacts. Piles of shoes. Gold watches. Buttons. A glass wall of names. I wrote down as many as I could in my sketchbook. Later, I counted twenty. We passed displays of pottery with valuables that prisoners had buried in the grounds of the camps and never returned to reclaim. We stepped through a dark room, which commemorated the lives of the lost children. In Israel, the Holocaust was more personal than it had been in Washington D.C. The history and hopes of this land were whispered to the German Jewish children at night when their parents tucked them to bed. To this land their thoughts wandered at night, as they, hungry and bruised, grasped warmth stacked on wooden boards. And here the survivors fought after the war, when the White Papers limited immigration. They travelled in boats meant to carry bananas, crowded on shelves, trying not to breathe too loudly. The British authorities intercepted and turned back most vessels. When the *Exodus 1937* arrived, carrying 4,500 Holocaust survivors, the British shipped the refugees back to Germany. Sometimes survivors were sent to detention camps on Cyprus, channeling Jews from concentration camps to displaced persons camps.

Outside Yad Vashem, the tough, no nonsense man who had been our tour guide for ten days

Culture Shock

described how his father was sent out of Germany as a child. We embraced each other as he began to tear up, describing how his father was reunited with his own mother years after.

When I was still too young to understand hatred, I found a video on Youtube that scared me. It was a children's program with a Mickey Mouse-like character singing with children in a classroom, "We will annihilate the Jews" and about marching into Jerusalem, setting it aflame, and celebrating. The mouse was named Farfour, an invention of Hamas. In the last episode, Farfour is beaten by Israeli "criminal despicable terrorists." A young girl explains, "He was martyred at the hand of the criminals, the murderers of innocent children."

I watched another video titled, "I'm Anti-Semitic" and read the comment section advocating the killing of Jews, until I became too upset. This, along with jokes about burning Jews in ovens, and a boy telling a Jewish girl in my grade to "get over" the Holocaust, led me to keep my Star of David necklace tucked under my shirt. Sometimes, when it pops out, and people ask "You're Jewish?", I flinch. I don't tell people I lived in Israel for a year.

Once I went to Smoothie King from sports practice, wearing a tank top that revealed the Star of David. The guy behind the counter asked, "You're Jewish?"

'Yes," I said, trying to pay quickly.

"Do you sanctify the tabernacle on Passover?"
"What?"
"Oh, so you don't celebrate holidays?" he said.
"I do," I said.
"We sanctify the tabernacle at my church on Passover," he said.
"What?" I said again, and the loop repeated for a few minutes.
"I'm sorry, I don't know what that is," I said, finally. I thanked him and grabbed my smoothie, relieved the conversation had gone in a more confusing direction than I had expected.

In 1948, the UN voted to partition Palestine, giving the Jews more than half of the land. Once the Mandate ended, David Ben-Gurion proclaimed the independence of Israel with the *Declaration of the Establishment of the state of Israel*:

> The State of Israel will be open for Jewish immigration and for the Ingathering of the Exiles; it will foster the development of the country for the benefit of all its inhabitants; it will be based on freedom, justice and peace as envisaged by the prophet of Israel; it will ensure complete equality of social and political rights to all its inhabitance irrespective of religion, race or sex; it will guarantee freedom of religion,

Culture Shock

conscience, language, education and
culture; it will safeguard the Holy Places
of all religions; and it will be faithful to
the principles of the Charter of the
United Nations.

To the Arab inhabitants of Israel, the document promised, "to preserve peace and participate in the upbuilding of the State on the basis of full and equal citizenship and due representation in all its provisional and permanent institutions."

That evening, Israel was attacked by Egypt, Transjordan, Syria, Lebanon, and Iraq. Israel won the war and gained territory in the Galilee and land formerly granted to the Palestinians in the United Nations resolution of 1947, which the Palestinians had refused to recognize. There are clear signs that Israel is surrounded by countries that want it gone. Once in awhile, a tour bus has to stop in the middle of the road so the police can remove a water bottle that could potentially be a bomb. In Israel, you can never pick something off the ground. Every suspicious looking bag must be inspected. At a museum, my family took the stairs because an elevator was filled with backpacks. Usually, you forget about these stops because they are infrequent and only minor annoyances.

My friends from Baltimore's sister city Ashkelon, who I know from my choir and from programs in Jewish Day School, are used to hearing sirens, warning about the impending rockets from Hamas in Gaza. Everyone stops what they are doing, whether they are sitting in a café, or playing soccer, to find the nearest bomb shelter. There is one in every building. A few years ago, Israel and Gaza went to war again, and for the first time in my life, Tel Aviv heard rockets. I was already in high school, so in my after-school Hebrew class, we watched videos of the confused people in Tel Aviv. They stood from their cafes sluggishly. Some ignored it. There is not a bomb shelter in every building in Tel Aviv, and most are used for storage. Our family friends from Beit Hashmonai[1] visited us in the United States. Their son, who is my age, told me that on their trip to Europe, every time a car alarm went off, he jumped, thinking it was a rocket.

After I left my Jewish Day School and entered the world of public school, people started asking me about Israel. "Isn't it dangerous? Are you going to be safe? Aren't you afraid of going there right now?"

I always say, "I feel safer in Israel than I do in the United States."

My principal in Israel was not wrong when he said that Baltimore was violent. Fifteen minutes from my house, teens get mugged and jumped, heroin addicts get high, and gunshots get mistaken for fireworks. In 2015, there were 344 homicides, and annually there are 8,499 violent crimes, 29,933

---

[1] A city half an hour from Tel Aviv

property crimes, and a total of 38,432 crimes. On the news, we hear about frequent shootings in schools, movie theatres, and malls. We lock the doors and set the alarm, even in daylight. My parents tried to make me take pepper spray when I went running as it started to get dark.

Israel was created to be a safe haven for the Jews, and it feels like one. The Iron Dome Missile Defense System, jointly funded with the United States, intercepts Hamas rockets before they can hit Israel. Every tour has a bodyguard with a gun. Every Israeli has army training, and the tourism programs know which areas are safe. Sites in Israel brim with smiling sightseers and beautiful landscapes. Unless you are traveling along the borders, you never see warning signs or barbed wire fences. Our friends never locked their door, and their neighbors invited themselves over. Teens stroll the streets at late hours, drifting between disco-techs and shopping centers. The streets are strung with lights, illuminating live bands and choirs, and the ocean calmly beats the shore. The only thing you really have to worry about is locking up your bike because theft is the most common crime.

The most dangerous threat to Israel takes place outside its borders. In Israel's perspective, Arab invasion and the need to protect Israel caused 700,000 Palestinian civilians to flee, some voluntarily and some forcibly, and become refugees after the War of Independence. To the Arab world, the establishment of Israel was an ethnic cleansing. After the Six-Day war, when Israel gained control the West Bank and Gaza Strip, Israel began to be seen as an "occupier." Some of the land used for current settlements in the West Bank was purchased by the Jewish National Fund. This land was lost to Jordan in the War of Independence, and all of the Jewish residents were forced to leave. An armistice agreement with Jordan, signed in April of 1949, established the present borders of the West Bank, which would be monitored by the UN. In 1950, Jordan formally annexed the West Bank, but only Pakistan and the United Kingdom recognized Jordan's occupation of the West Bank as legitimate. Neither this agreement nor the 1949 Armistice Agreements between Israel and Egypt, Lebanon, and Syria, required the Arabs to recognize Israel, or either side to give up claims to the territory on the border. Only after 1967, when the Palestinians lost the West Bank in the Six-Day-War, did the Palestinians support the borders. Jordan's King Hussein gave the West Bank to the Palestinians in 1988, but at this point, it did not belong to him.

In 1975, the United Nations passed a resolution calling Zionism a form of racism. The Israeli Ambassador to the UN noted the irony that the resolution was released on the thirty-seventh anniversary of Kristallnacht, when Nazis vandalized Jewish property, bashed the windows of Jewish storefronts, and burned prayer books and Torahs before the Holocaust. Martin Luther King responded,

"When people criticize Zionists, you meant Jews. That's Anti-Semitism."

The resolution was revoked in 1991, but Zionism is once again being equated with racism. Even my Jewish friends are posting articles about the selectivity of Zionism. During Israeli Apartheid Week, which criticizes Israel for "racist apartheid policies" and the "supremacy of Jews ethnic identity," one article in the *Columbia Spectator* stated, "we had been raised in a community that failed to face the anti-democratic reality of the State of Israel... We needed a community that taught its children that particularistic ethnonationalism and Jewish exceptionalism have no place in Judaism..."

In 1945, the Arab League began boycotting Jewish goods from British Mandate Palestine. In 1948, the boycott was expanded to include all countries that conducted trade with Israel. In 2005, The Boycott, Divestment, and Sanctions movement (BDS) was signed into action by the Council of National and Islamic Forces in Palestine, which included Hamas and two other organizations[2] listed as Designated Foreign Terrorist Organizations by the United States Department of States. According to its website, the BDS movement "works to end international support for Israel's oppression of Palestinians and pressure Israel to comply with international law." The

---

[2] Popular Front for the Liberation of Palestine (PFLP) and PFLP – General Command

movement finds many of its supporters on liberal college campuses. Recently, the platform of Black Lives Matter added a clause about the oppression of Palestine by Israel, calling it genocide.

In March 2015, The UN claimed that Israel was the worst human rights violator, with four resolutions on Israel, and only one on North Korea, Syria, and Iran. In January 2017, the United Nations Security Council allowed a resolution to pass declaring all Israeli settlements in the West Bank and east Jerusalem to be illegal. The United States, Israel's strongest ally, abstained from voting. Secretary of State John Kerry agreed with this assertion in his speech criticizing Israel's activity in the West Bank.

Award winning author, Matti Friedman wrote, "a distaste for Israel has come to be something between an acceptable prejudice and a prerequisite for entry… a belief that to some extent the Jews of Israel are a symbol of the world's ills, particularly those connected to nationalism, militarism, colonialism, and racism." Organizations in Palestinian territories tend to be heavily pro-Palestine and anti-Israel, which causes reporters and editors covering Israel to make editorial decisions of the same nature. In 2008, the Associated Press Jerusalem bureau suppressed a report about an Israeli peace offer to Palestine. Hamas's build-up of military weapons in Gaza and a rally at Al-Quds University, featuring dead Israeli soldiers and salutes in support of Islamic Jihad, were not covered.

Culture Shock

The media has taken a role of political activism that, with its role as a gatekeeper, affects how the world sees Israel. As stated by Friedman, "For the international press, the uglier characteristics of Palestinian politics and society are mostly untouchable because they would disrupt the Israel story, which is a story of Jewish moral failure." In 2000, Israel accepted a plan for peace under President Bill Clinton, which the Palestinians rejected. However, this event was depicted as being entirely Israel's fault. I once read a story that described an IDF soldier attacking a Palestinian woman, excluding the detail that the woman had tried to stab the soldier with a knife.

Readers believe that Israel is an oppressor, but this is the only side of the story that the media shows. Hamas is aware of this. By storing weapons in Palestinian civilian structures like schools, hospitals, and homes, the organization induces Israel to strike areas that are intentionally designed to kill civilians, making sure that these events are filmed so that the rest of the world can become outraged with Israel. "It is easier just to leave the other photographers out of the frame and let the picture tell the story: Here are dead people, and Israel killed them," Friedman wrote. Hamas continues to send its own rockets from the cover of Palestinian civilians. In the summer of 2014, this caused the death of many Palestinians.

There is no doubt that the Palestinians are oppressed. Life is terrible for them. They are caught in a war between two opposing governments who wants the other gone, no matter who is right. This, along with propaganda provided by Hamas, causes an intense hatred of Israel and hostility toward Jews. In Egypt, from 1882-1924, Jews were attacked in anti-foreigner riots. In 1948, 2,000 Jews were arrested and had their property confiscated. Explosions in the Jewish quarter of Cairo explosion in the Jewish Quarter killed more than 70 Jews and injured 200, as homes were looted and the government seized property. In 1956, 25,000 Jews were expelled from Egypt. In 1960, synagogues, Jewish orphanages, elderly homes, and hospitals were shut down. In 1967, Jewish Egyptian officials were fired, with 500 arrested, tortured, and held for three years. Others were stripped of their citizenship and expelled.

Hamas' Charter declares, "Israel will rise and will remain erect until Islam eliminates it as it had eliminated its predecessors," and, "Israel, by virtue of its being Jewish and of having a Jewish population, defies Islam and the Muslims." It claims that after coveting Palestine, the Zionists will expand "from the Nile to the Euphrates," and will progress onward to more expansion, a scheme "laid out in the *Protocols of the Elders of Zion*." A two-state solution cannot be possible if Hamas and other organizations of the Arab nations will only be satisfied with Israel's destruction.

What the media doesn't tell you is that Israel is raising funds for humanitarian aid in Syria and giving refuge to the children of Aleppo. Israel is responsible for developing essential medicines and technologies, such as the ApiFix system to fix sever spine curvature and an MRI device that destroys tumors without surgery. What the media doesn't show is my eighth grade class visit to an Arab school within Israel. The kids approached us with roses and walked us around the school, arm and arm, without a slight bit of awkwardness that we were Jewish and they were Arab. San Diego student Erin Gonzalez thought that Israel was "akin to apartheid" until she visited and realized that Israel accepted all religions and cultures. She was surprised to learn that although the settlements were condemned by the UN, many Palestinians were employed in industrial zones and received government benefits in the Israeli settlements. Israeli-Arab women serve in parliament and hold positions in business, trade, arts, and entertainment. Organizations such as the Jasmine Conference and the Center for Jewish-Arab Economic Development focus on Israel-Arab integration, especially concerning the empowerment of Arab women.

Mohammad S. Dajani Daoudi, an ex-guerrilla fighter of the PLO, changed his opinion on Israel, after his father received cancer treatment in an Israeli hospital, and Israeli doctors and soldiers cared for his mother during her death. In 2007, he founded the organization Wasatia, which promotes compromise and nonviolence, as taught in Muslim tradition. Although not part of Palestinian curriculum, he teaches students in the West Bank about the Holocaust and took the first group of Palestinian students to visit the Auschwitz-Birkenau State Museum in Poland. The program also sends Israeli students to a Palestinian refugee camp in Bethlehem. Faced with condemnation by Palestinian universities, Daoudi continued to teach and lead trips, as he said, "It helped emphasize the human story of the Holocaust, to study the meaning of the historical narrative as related to our conflict, to heighten empathy, awareness, and sensitivity."

Empathy, awareness, and sensitivity are needed now. Despite some discomfort, I have never feared being Jewish in the United States. Since Donald Trump became president, I see more swastikas these days and "Make America White Again" graffiti. His campaign was founded on fear, and his presidency is too. The Alt Right, a white supremacist group laden with racism and anti-Semitism, is rising.

On February 28th, 2017, the Owings Mills JCC received a bomb threat, one of over fifty Jewish Community Centers to receive bomb threats in the last two months. This was the same building where I attended preschool, joined a basketball team, and performed with my chapter of the HaZamir choir every year. My cousins' Jewish day school in Rockville was also evacuated due to a bomb threat. Hate crimes against Jews have increased this year. A Chabad synagogue in Orlando, Florida was vandalized on Rosh Hashanah, with "Free Palestine" spray-painted on its front sign. In early February, a group of subway riders boarded to find swastikas and comments like "Jews belong in the ovens" scrawled on every window of the subway. Within two minutes, the subway riders had cleaned off the windows with hand sanitizer and tissues.

I'm scared. Next year, I am going to college and the Boycott, Divestment, and Sanctions movement is spreading on campuses. At Goucher College, ten minutes from my house, a group of student BDS supporters protested an Israeli lecturer. The lecturer asked a girl from the movement if they could talk about their differences. An adult ushered her away, prohibiting her from speaking to the man. Silent hate steams like a kettle with its lid sealed as people refuse to listen or speak to each other. My Star of David necklace remains tucked beneath my shirt.

While I was working on this essay on January 8th, 2017, four Israeli soldiers were killed and sixteen injured in Jerusalem when a Palestinian rammed his car into pedestrians on the sidewalk. The media remained conveniently silent. I am helpless in defending my homeland. A friend once interviewed me about the Israeli-Palestinian conflict. True, I did not know everything that I know now about the conflict, but I offered truth. She did not believe a word I said. Israelis are loud and feed you too much, and they smoke in public places, but they don't want violence.

I am not trying to change your opinion on the Israeli-Palestinian conflict. I offer facts for you to piece together how you choose. If you get anything out of this essay without thinking that I am wrong, or being unfair, consider this: as soon as Israeli soldiers graduate from high school, they enter the IDF. Next year, the new recruits will be my rambunctious sixth grade class from Israel. They will be my friends from HaZamir. Before our performance in Carnegie Hall last year, the seniors in the Israeli chapters stood on stage and sang The Prayer for the State of Israel, in an arrangement by David Burger titled simply "Tfilah," or "prayer":

> Our Father in Heaven, Rock and Redeemer of Israel, bless the State of Israel…Strengthen the hands of those who defend our holy land, grant them deliverance, and adorn them in a mantle of victory. Ordain peace in the land and grant its inhabitants eternal happiness.

With each phrase, the music ascends until the choir is soaring, as if our words could stir our silent God, and He could awaken long enough to grant us peace. I can never sing along because my throat tightens up. Everyone cries and embraces one another. A Jewish homeland means a safe haven, a reassurance that the Holocaust cannot happen again, even if America becomes ridden with anti-Semitic hate organizations, even if the BDS movement succeeds in cutting Israel from its strongest ally. About 8,000 Jews immigrated to Israel last year, welcomed by "Heveinu Shalom Aleichem." Following the Charlie Hebdo attack, and two days later, the kosher supermarket attack that killed four Jews, they fled France, where synagogues were being burned; people feared wearing their yarmulkes in public. This time, they could leave before it was too late.

Where I'm From

Every year from seventh grade to ninth grade, my English class imitated the poem "Where I'm From," by George Ella Lyon. Over and over, we analyzed the structure and the imagery and filled out worksheets on our favorite foods, colloquialisms, and religious passages.

Today, mine would go something like this:

I am from stocked pantries, running water, pet dogs, two guinea pigs, and a fish.

I am from my biggest responsibilities being feeding the guinea pigs, cleaning my room, and taking out the trash and recycling.

I am from Jewish Day School, Peabody piano lessons, and summer camp.

I am from pretending to be squirrels, digging in the pine cone patterned rug in the living room with my siblings, spreading our blankets in the hallway and riding magic carpets, from building forts with couch cushions.

I am from the inevitable injury or tantrum of one of my siblings.

Culture Shock

    I am from fighting and slamming the doors of our separate bedrooms.

    I am from geniuses.

    I am from the unknown.

    I am from suddenness, tectonic shifts in our worlds.

    I am from crumbled papers under lamplight.

    I am from my mother driving three kids to three different schools, from my father opening the refrigerator to make food puns after a long day at work.

    I am from the love my parents gave to me, from these stories they told me when I came to them, crying that I didn't have friends, worried that I wouldn't get into college.

My great grandfather had a photographic memory and was the most brilliant man his teachers, wife, and sons had ever met. His son Manny went to Harvard Medical School, became a famous doctor, and wrote *Rubin's Pathology Clinicopathologic Foundations of Medicine*, one of the most used medical textbooks in the world. His son Moe was a professional musician and published essays and poetry in English, Spanish, Italian, and French. Almost all of Yaacov's sons attended Columbia University and obtained medical or law degrees from Harvard.

    Sophie Greenberg's half brother, Max, had a son named Jack. Jack Greenberg succeeded Thurgood Marshall as the NAACP Legal Defense and Educational Fund's Director-Counsel. He was the youngest member of a team of lawyers to argue *Brown v. Board of Education* before the Supreme Court. The case overturned the "separate but equal" doctrine of segregated public schools. He worked with Martin Luther King Jr. to eliminate racial restriction in public parks and discrimination in health care. In 2001, he was awarded a Presidential Citizens Medal. President Clinton said, "in the courtroom and the classroom, Jack Greenberg has been a crusader for freedom and equality for more than half a century."

I can't help but wonder if intelligence diminishes through the generations as I procrastinate on my homework with Netflix and struggle to write a sentence with the words in the right order.

Abba thought my father was a protégé. Before he could talk, Avi knew the alphabet. Carol's graduate advisor didn't believe it until Avi demonstrated by pointing to the letters. By the time he was three, Avi was solving math problems. When he was four or five, he was doing geometry, trigonometry, algebra, and physics, which Abba taught him from a twelfth grade book. At six years old, Avi learned to read in three days. Abba's brother Manny, impossible to impress, watched Abba teach Avi and said, "He's a genius."[1]

My father, on the other hand, remembers being a normal kid. On the kibbutz, he and the other kids played games outside. Somebody noticed that he

---

[1] "The way he learned was like Mozart with music," Zayde said.

was fast, so Avi ran everywhere he went because he thought he could outrun anyone. It felt like a superpower.

When they moved to Haifa, Abba and Carol let their children roam freely. Avi walked to school with his best friend Zvi Cohen, who lived in the apartment below and was in the same school and grade. [2] Avi played at a friend's house and was hit in the eye with a tennis ball. He went home and found the door to the apartment locked. He sat by the door and cried until his parents came home and took him to the hospital, where he spent the night.

An American childhood is different from an Israeli one. I was never let out of my parents' sight. When I was three, my father and I went on a walk in the winter with our dog, Mendl. I was holding the leash when Mendl began to run. I fell on the ice and watched the blood flow from my fingernail, which had become slightly detached from my pinky. My dad immediately rushed me to the hospital, where I got stitches. My parents helped feed me because my hand was wrapped in gauze for a week.

Avi spoke English at home with his parents, but he was an Israeli kid. He spoke Hebrew fluently and played soccer in the concrete lot outside of the apartment building in the dark, scraping his knees and elbows and not caring. There were cats everywhere,

---

[2] Zvi died at the age of twenty two in a mountain climbing accident.

and he pet them and brought them milk. He liked
snails. He put them on his arm and watched them
crawl on him.

His family took trips in their white station
wagon, which had rear facing backseats. The children
always fought about sitting in the back, but my father
can't remember it if was because they wanted to or
didn't want to. They visited Jerusalem, Tel Aviv, the
Kinneret, Jaffa, the Galilee, and the beach, places that
were cheap and close because the family had no money.
Avi was scared of water. He wore large floaties on his
arms and refused to go too deep. He didn't learn how
to swim until his family moved to Birmingham.

For my siblings and me, it was the middle seat.
On road trips in Israel, we stood outside our small
silver car, fighting over who had to sit in the middle.
And now, with all of us in high school, we still argue,
though more passive aggressively, over the middle seat.

My mother's paternal grandfather, Henry Wolok, was
born on March 21st, 1912 in Vladimirets, USSR. He left
for America and met New York native Henrietta
Singer. They married in Michigan, in March of 1936
and had sons Mitchell and Lawrence, my grandfather.

My other great grandfather Alexander Frank,
whom my sister Tamara Alexandra is named after, was
born in Austria-Hungary in 1908. He fled to America
after facing persecution and married a woman named
Ann, who was born in Palestine. They had two
daughters: Barbara and Maureen, my grandmother.

Culture Shock

Alexander was a stern father, and Maureen felt sad when he yelled at her. Ann Frank died from breast cancer at around forty years old. Maureen was fourteen.

Larry Wolok and Maureen Frank met at a dance in Michigan. In 1968, they had my mother Ann. Her parents divorced when she was three. Ann grew up in Oak Park, Michigan with her mother and older brother, Mark. As the provider for the family, Maureen worked full time at a hospital as an EKG technician. Every morning, Ann was dropped off at her grandparents' house in Southfield, which was close to the school bus stop. Preschool days were short, and she ate lunch at her grandparents.

Ann had almost no rules. She considered herself a tomboy. She fought often with her brother, didn't play with dolls, and spent time outside with the other children on her street, throwing footballs, playing tag, or riding her bike.

In kindergarten, she attended Hillel Day School in Farmington Hills. Her mother left for work before the school bus came for Ann. She was the first one to be picked up, so it took an hour to get to school. Once in the winter, she slipped on ice as she was walking to the bus and got a bruise. She went back inside and skipped school because her mother wasn't home.

Her brother Mark had been an entrepreneur from a young age as the neighborhood's paperboy. Ann also wanted to make money. She bought whistle pops in bulk, brought them to school, and sold them for more money than she paid. After her brother stopped delivering newspapers, she took over his paper route. Every week, the newspapers were delivered to her front door, and she rolled up each paper, tied a rubber band around it, and tossed it into a bag on her bike. She rode around the neighborhood and threw newspapers on the front porches. Her friends were hired to help roll the papers and she gave them each a dollar from her salary.

Ann's clothing was from Kmart, one of many reasons she felt out of place in private school. Occasionally, she slept at the home of her aunt Barbara, who was a kindergarten teacher at Hillel. Barbara brought bags of hand-me-downs for Ann to take home, which was embarrassing. In fifth grade, she played house with her two best friends. Adam was the husband, Betsy was the wife, and they told Ann to be the dog. Ann told her mother she wanted to go to public school for sixth grade.

Her brother was already in junior high, so Ann walked to school alone. One boy hated her, and she didn't understand why. He tried to convince one of the bigger girls in their grade to beat Ann up. The girl wouldn't do it, so he teased Ann and hit her. Finally, Ann slapped him hard across the face. She had been a better student at Hillel. In public school, she started getting Bs and even Cs.

Every other weekend, she visited her father, who had moved back in with his parents on Pontiac

Lake. He was like a kid who never grew up. He had two motorcycles and every kind of boat imaginable: a sailboat, a rowboat, a paddle-boat, pontoon, and a ski boat. He gave his children BB guns. There were many hills nearby, and they went hiking. His brother Mitchell had three girls, and every summer the two younger girls spent a few weeks at the lake house with their grandparents, uncle, and cousins. They made forts in their bunk beds. They played monopoly, croquet, and badminton. In the vegetable garden, they picked cucumbers to pickle. Ann's grandmother made specialty dishes: cabbage rolls with meat and homemade mac and cheese. In the winter, they rode her father's two snowmobiles and skated on the frozen lake. Her father led cross-country ski trips for the YMCA, and he bought his children ski outfits and took them with him.

Returning to her mother was a sharp contrast. With no financial support from her ex-husband, Maureen was bitter. In sixth grade, Ann said a bad word to her mother, and her mother washed her mouth out with soap. Sent to her room as punishment, Ann sometimes snuck out the door that led to the backyard, and hid behind the shed, or climbed the apple tree. One time, she climbed the tree, and her mother grabbed hold of her leg and pulled her down. Another time, her punishment was that she had to stay home from school. Ann went to school anyway, and her mother came to her class, made a scene, and told Ann to leave. These behaviors occurred especially after

Ann and her brother returned from their father's house. Ann reacted by cursing at her mother. In response, Maureen pulled her by the hair.

Avi didn't know any other American community outside of Birmingham, so he thought the rest of America was just like it. The Jewish community was tight-knit. In the first graduating class of the Jewish Day School, there were six kids in his grade. Avi exchanged letters with one of his friends from Israel. Shortly after the Rubins arrived to Birmingham, a girl from Avi's class in Israel died in a car crash.

Avi was fluent in Hebrew, so his father arranged for the principal of the school, who was also the rabbi, to tutor him in Tanakh. While his peers got to be social in their classes, he had to sit alone with the rabbi. In his math class, the students worked at their own levels, which meant that some of the students learned with the younger kids. Avi was at a high school level, and they didn't know what to do with him. He already knew the information in the high school math workbooks they gave him. He found his classes boring, and he was always being reprimanded because he couldn't stop talking. But he loved gym and recess, where he threw footballs with his friends and played sports with the athletic kids in the grade below them.

After school, Avi played on the JCC soccer team, which was in the same building. His parents didn't drive him around, so he could only participate if he could find a ride. He knew all of the Jewish kids in

Culture Shock

his community from camp, synagogue, and ballroom dancing, which was customary in the south. Boys had to wear ties, and girls wore white gloves. The boys and girls were separated into two rooms. When a boy asked a girl to dance, they entered a third room where they learned ballroom moves. Many girls were a head taller than Avi. He once danced with the tallest girl, and everyone got a kick out of it. He thought it was funny too.

After ballroom, everyone went to Pasquale's Pizza. A quarter bought them three songs from the Jukebox. They played the Bee Gees, Huey Lewis and the News, and "Bad Case of Loving You," by Robert Palmer over and over. Avi was picky (only eating plain spaghetti, bread with peanut butter, dry cereal, chocolate milk, mustard, apples, bananas, oranges, watermelon, and apricots), so he didn't eat at these gatherings. One day his father offered him five dollars if he could finish one of his mother's hamburgers. Five dollars was a lot of money. He took a jar of peanut butter, covered the hamburger with it, and took little bites so he couldn't taste the meat. He got the five dollars

Three months before Avi's Bar Mitzvah, his family moved to Nashville. All of his classmates threw huge Bar Mitzvah celebrations at country clubs. Avi was at an awkward age and had a late birthday, so he was younger than all of his classmates. Furthermore, he was on scholarship at the University School of Nashville, which was filled with rich Jewish kids who had known each other from kindergarten. Like Ann, his clothes were from Kmart specials, he didn't have money, and he didn't wear matching socks. He was good at math, so everyone picked on him. He got along with a popular African American boy who joked around with him in Spanish class, but he was the only one. Two kids came to Avi's Bar Mitzvah party.

His class started a soccer unit in PE. The gym teacher chose two captains to pick teams. The first player picked was Juan Carlos from El Salvador. After all of the girls, the last person picked was Avi, who sat there thinking, *I'm gonna show them.* He ended up on Juan Carlos' team.

"I'm really good," Avi told him. Juan Carlos was skeptical, but they began passing the ball down the field. They dribbled past everyone. After a few minutes, the score was ten to nothing.[3]

The coach soon placed Avi and Juan Carlos on different teams. After class, the gym teacher took Avi to a high school Spanish class. The teacher, a woman named Barb, was the coach of the varsity soccer team.

"I think I just found someone for your team," the coach said.

"Really?" she said.

"You should see him play." She agreed to watch him during PE.

---

[3] "American kids don't know how to play soccer," my father says.

Culture Shock

Avi played on the varsity high school soccer team in eighth grade and ninth grade. Fifteen schools crammed into the gym for indoor tournaments. Avi was a starter. Although he was tiny, he was fast. The team advanced to the semifinals. At one point, the gym started chanting his jersey number "Go number four!" He scored a goal, and the crowd cheered. His teammates picked him up and carried him around the gym.

Still, he hated ninth grade. After breaking down crying in the kitchen, his parents switched him to the public high school, Hillwood. Despite warnings that there were no Jews, kids got beaten up, and he would never survive, Avi loved it. He found people who were more like him and met his good friend, Karl.

At sixteen, he began working at Krystal's, and because his eating habits made him uncomfortable in social situations, he forced himself to eat french fries. He began "hamburger training," which involved taking a big bun with a tiny piece of meat and lathering it with mustard. He got shivers and felt sick just thinking about the meat, but he ate a little more every day until he could eat an entire hamburger.

Avi's parents were stricter than most of his friends'. When Avi asked to go to a school football game, they said no. When he asked to go to the movies, they almost always said no. It usually came down to money. Sometimes his parents asked him to leave the room, and he could hear his mother trying to convince his father to let him go. His father still said no. His parents never came to his games and thought he exaggerated details about his team picking him up on their shoulders.

During his sophomore year, his soccer team advanced to the quarterfinals of a tournament. When games went into overtime, the teams played for five minutes. If no goals were made, they played for another minute, and with each passing minute, a player was taken off each team. Avi scored the majority of the goals and was designated number one. The score was two-two when the game went into overtime. It came down to a shootout between Avi and the best player on the other team. He came at Avi with the ball. Avi ran, stuck his foot out, kicked the ball away, and dribbled it all the way down the field. His opponent chased after him, and as he was about to catch him, Avi took the shot. The shot landed in the middle of the net. His team picked him up on their shoulders and the crowd cheered.

The coach drove Avi home and asked his parents if he could come in. They gathered in the living room, and the coach summed up the game and said it was a shame they weren't there. Abba didn't appreciate being told to come to games. Again, Avi asked himself why they weren't interested in his soccer.

Maureen remarried when in the spring of 1980, when Ann was twelve. Ann's brother Michael was born in December of the same year. Maureen's new husband was wealthy, with a master's degree in international business. He had retired from Chrysler and sent out his resume to various countries and took an offer in Mexico. In the summer of 1980, Ann moved to a small town called Querétaro. They stayed in a hotel for a few months. They went swimming horseback riding every day. Because Maureen was pregnant and needed to be near a major hospital, they moved to a mini mansion in the city of Loma Linda, a suburb of Mexico City. Ann's stepfather had to commute two hours between Mexico City and Querétaro.

Ann and Mark took a bus to the American school. Sometimes, a driver took them and picked them up at the end of the day. They attended a synagogue near her home, and Ann prepared for her Bat Mitzvah with the rabbi. She liked him because she reminded him of his granddaughter. Most of the children at her school were the children of embassy workers and wealthy Mexicans who could afford the tuition, and there were other Jewish kids.

This was not the case when she moved back to the States. Maureen decided she didn't want to live in Mexico anymore, and they moved to Minnesota. Ann went back to public high school and was the only Jew after her brother graduated. The kids were not friendly and had never met a Jew before. Once a boy she thought she was friends with drew a swastika on his desk. There was another boy who called her "Warlock" because her last name was Wolok.

Ann had to walk to school, which was eight blocks away. In the winter, her mother never checked if the school was closed. Sometimes, Ann arrived at school to find that it was a snow day and had to walk back. Her mother didn't pick her up. Maureen gave all of her attention to Michael, who was at home. Ann couldn't wait to leave home.

Avi and his friend Karl applied to Cornell, with the intention of becoming roommates. Although Avi's family was poor, his parents told their kids that in choosing a college, money wasn't a factor. Karl got into Cornell, but Avi didn't. He ended up at the University of Michigan.

For the first time in his life, Avi became a serious student. His was pre-med for one semester. He got a job in the cancer research lab, where he took mice out of dirty drawers, cleaned and filled the drawers with sawdust, and dropped the mice by the tail back into the clean drawer. Inside the lab, he pulled whole mouse intestines from jars, stretched, cleaned, and strained them out, and laid them on the table for testing. The job paid three dollars and 35 cents per hour. He worked four-hour shifts once or twice a week. On top of this, he took six courses, got five As, and a B plus in chemistry. He decided he didn't want to be pre-med. For one, he hated chemistry, and second, he had fallen in love with computer science.

Ann's brother and cousins went to the University of Michigan. This was the only school Ann applied to.

Culture Shock

When she visited the university, an admissions counselor told Ann that she was not going to get in, even though was in the top ten of her class. She applied with her stepfather's information, which made her ineligible for financial aid because of his income. Her stepfather offered to pay for college, but Maureen wouldn't let him. Ann had saved up ten thousand dollars between her Bat Mitzvah money, gifts, and paychecks. She used most of the money her first year of college for books, room, and board. The next year, she took Federal Work-Study jobs and a Pell Grant and was able to put herself through school without any help. Her mother and stepfather got divorced when she was in college.

Avi was the happiest he'd ever been. He attended almost all of the football games, played intramural soccer, and left his job at the cancer research lab for the computer center. He sat at a desk, took people's IDs, and sent them to stations. He worked for three hours every day and did his homework when he didn't have to monitor or change the ink in the printers. In graduate school, he was promoted to consultant and got his own office.

Ann realized she didn't know how to study in college. Her dorm was in a hall notorious for partying. They went out three or four nights a week to bars. After receiving her first C since sixth grade and ending the first grading period with a GPA of 2.8, she decided she had to get serious. She graduated with a 3.2. She always got As in the classes she liked, like writing. Wanting to go into sales at Michigan's business school, Ann took marketing, economics, and accounting, had a hard time, and realized business school was not for her. Then she took Freedom of Speech, a constitutional law course. She began taking philosophy and journalism classes. She took Juvenile Justice and tutored kids who were in juvy. Before graduating, she had to decide between a career in journalism or law school. She decided to go into an occupation where she could support herself. In law, she could go into practice on her own. She didn't have to work for anybody.

Avi was at the top of his class, but in graduate school, he was astounded by the intelligence of his peers. He needed a 3.9 GPA to get into the PhD program, and he was just below that. In the summer between his fourth and fifth year at grad school, his friend Steven Stryk set him up on a blind date with his cousin, Ann Wolok. Ann's father remarried around the same time as Maureen remarried. His new wife had converted to Judaism and didn't want children because she was scared of childbirth. Until she graduated from the University of Detroit Mercy School of Law, Ann lived with her father and stepmother, who made her pay rent and clean the bathrooms. Ann called her "her step-witch." Her father and stepmother also got divorced.

Culture Shock

Her aunt, Barbara, nicknamed "Ms. Matchmaker," tried to set her up with guys she met as a kindergarten teacher. Ann went on a few dates and decided not to trust Barbara's judgment again. Barbara's son Steven told Ann that he thought she would like his friend Avi.

They met at a restaurant. Avi was already there when Ann arrived. After dinner, Avi asked if she wanted to stay for a drink.

"I'll call you," he said, as he walked her to her car.

"I hope you do," Ann responded.

Ann and Avi started dating the summer before her last year of law school. They moved to Ann Arbor together around Thanksgiving time. After her finals, they got engaged.

They were married in New Jersey on December 18th, 1994. Three years later, they got a little white Bichon Havanese, whom they named Mendl, after the rabbi who married them. On March 20th, 1999, at 12:03 in the morning, they had a baby girl, whom they named Elana Molly Rubin. On her birth announcement, they wrote "Future graduate of the University of Michigan, class of 2021." In 2002, they had twins: Tamara Alexandra Rubin and Benny Charles Rubin, born five minutes apart.

When Elana was three and the twins were five and a half months old, the family moved to Baltimore. The children spent the summers outside with the neighborhood kids. In the fall, they attended Jewish day school, like their parents had dreamed. Every spring, they flew to Nashville for Passover with the family. The cousins played together, pantomime games about princesses and burger joints, which throughout the years, turned to giggles about boys in the corner.

When Elana was in fifth grade and the twins in second, they sat down for a family meeting in the living room. Within a few months, they were packing for Israel. The day before they moved, Elana sat by her bedroom window with her journal. She touched her palm to the glass and looked over her lawn. The clouds seemed far away and large, as they slowly spun around her, until the edge of the furthest cloud was out of view. She felt infinite and small.

Notes

Culture Shock

"Israeli Slang 101." *Israel on the House*. Sachlav Group, 21 Oct. 2015. Web. 04 Mar. 2017.

Leichman, Abigail Klein. "Israel's Top 45 Greatest Inventions of All Time." *Israel21c.org*. Salamandra, 26 Sept. 2011. Web. 04 Mar. 2017.

Everything Under the Sun

JPS Hebrew-English Tanakh: The Traditional Hebrew Text and the New JPS Translation. Philadelphia: Jewish Publication Society, 2003. Print.

Long Lost

Dykman, JT. "WWII Soviet Experience." *Eisenhowerinstitute.org*. The Eisenhower Institute at Gettysburg College, Web. 01 Apr. 2017.

History.com Staff. "Cold War History." History.com. A&E Television Networks, 2009. Web. 01 Apr. 2017.

Glenn, Susan A. "The Jewish Cold War: Anxiety and Identity in the Aftermath of the Holocaust." *David W. Belin Lecture in American Jewish Affairs*. Michigan Publishing, University of Michigan Library, 01 Jan. 1970. Web. 28 Mar. 2017.

"Jews in Former Soviet Union." *Jewish Virtual Library*. American-Israeli Cooperative Enterprise. Web. 01 Apr. 2017.

"Joseph Stalin." *Jewish Virtual Library*. American-Israeli Cooperative Enterprise. Web. 01 Apr. 2017.

Jew-ish

Greenberg, Sidney, and Jonathan D. Levine. *Siddur á ̦¥adash: Worship, Study, and Song for Sabbath and Festival Mornings =*. New York, NY: Prayer Book, 2007. Print.

"Jewish Sects and Movements." *ReligionFacts.com.* 21 Nov. 2016. Web. Accessed 4 Mar. 2017.

"Orthodox Judaism Today." *My Jewish Learning*. Web. 27 Feb. 2017.

Steinberg, Rabbi Paul. "What Is Shemini Atzeret?" *My Jewish Learning*. Kveller, JTA, Jewniverse, 70/FacesMedia. Web. 29 Mar. 2017.

"The Origins of Reform Judaism." *Jewishvirtuallibrary.org*. Jewish Virtual Library. Web. 04 Mar. 2017.

A Body of Land

Admin. "Praying Together in Jerusalem Unites Christians, Muslims and Jews." *Elijah Interfaith*. Elijah-Interfaith.com, 23 May 2016. Web. 04 Apr. 2017.

Alkhateeb, Firas. "How the British Divided Up the Arab World." *Lostislamichistory.com*. Lost Islamic History, 15 Dec. 2015. Web. 04 Mar. 2017.

Barnavi, Eli. "Jewish Immigration to Pre-State Israel." *Myjewishlearning.com*. 70 Faces Media, n.d. Web. 04 Mar. 2017.

Bajekal, Naina. "Israel-Palestinian Clash: 6 Things to Know about Jerusalem." *Time*. Time, 13 Oct. 2015. Web. 04 Apr. 2017.

"British Palestine Mandate: History & Overview." *Jewishvirtuallibrary.org*. American-Israeli Cooperative Enterprise. Web. 04 Mar. 2017.

Gradstein, Linda. "East Jerusalem's Identity Crisis." *The Jerusalem Post | JPost.com*. Jpost Inc., 4 Oct. 2012. Web. 04 Apr. 2017.

"History of Jewish Immigration to Israel (Aliyah)." *ReformJudaism.org*. Union for Reform Judaism, 17 Aug. 2016. Web. 04 Apr. 2017.

Steve. "Israel: A Melting Pot of Cultures." *IsraelSeen.com*. IsraelSeen.com, 29 May 2012. Web. 04 Apr. 2017.

The Learning Network. "Nov. 29, 1947 | U.N. Partitions Palestine, Allowing for Creation of Israel." *The New York Times*. The New York Times, 29 Nov. 2011. Web. 04 Mar. 2017.

Aliyah

Brown, O'Brien. "The Arab-Israeli War of 1973: Honor, Oil, and Blood." *HistoryNet*. HistoryNet, 30 Dec. 2015. Web. 28 Feb. 2017.

History.com Staff. "Yom Kippur War." *History.com*. A&E Television Networks, 2009. Web. 28 Feb. 2017.

Rabinovich, Abraham. "Three Years Too Late, Golda Meir Understood How War Could Have Been Avoided." *The*

Times of Israel. The Times of Israel, 12 Sept. 2013. Web. 28 Feb. 2017.

The Invention of the Wheel

DHWTY. "The Revolutionary Invention of the Wheel." *Ancient Origins*. Ancient Origins, 2 June 2014. Web. 04 Mar. 2017.

Gambino, Megan. "A Salute to the Wheel." *Smithsonian.com*. Smithsonian Institution, 17 June 2009. Web. 04 Mar. 2017.

"Gilad Shalit." *Jewishvirtuallibrary.org*. American-Israeli Cooperative Enterprise. Web. 12 Mar. 2017.

"Historical Timeline: 1900-Present - Israeli-Palestinian Conflict - ProCon.org." *Procon.org*. Procon.org, 22 July 2015. Web. 04 Mar. 2017.

"IDF Seizes PA Weapons Ship: The Karine A Affair." *Jewishvirtuallibrary.org*. American- Israeli Cooperative Enterprise. Web. 12 Mar. 2017.

"Intifada Begins on Gaza Strip." *History.com*. A&E Television Networks. Web. 06 Mar. 2017.

JPS Tanakh: The Jewish Bible. Place of Publication Not Identified: Jewish Publication Society, 1991. Print.

Laub, Zachary. "Hamas." *Council on Foreign Relations*. Council on Foreign Relations, 1 Aug. 2014. Web. 11 Mar. 2017. <http://www.cfr.org/israel/hamas/p8968>.

Marshall, Jonathan. "The US Hand in the Syrian Mess." *Consortiumnews.com*. Consortiumnews, 20 July 2015. Web. 12 Mar. 2017.

Plen, Matt. "Baruch Goldstein." *My Jewish Learning*. 70 Faces Media.Web. 11 Mar. 2017.

Raiciu, Tudor. "History of the Wheel." *Autoevolution.com*. Autoevolution, 02 June 2009. Web. 04 Mar. 2017.

"The Negotiations | Shattered Dreams of Peace." *PBS*. Public Broadcasting Service. Web. 11 Mar. 2017.

Wilson, Scott. "Hamas Sweeps Palestinian Elections, Complicating Peace Efforts in Mideast." *The Washington Post*. WP Company, 27 Jan. 2006. Web. 12 Mar. 2017.

Woodford, Chris. "History of Cars: The Story of Automobiles from Prehistory to Today." *Explainthatstuff.com*. Explain That Stuff, 13 Nov. 2016. Web. 04 Mar. 2017.

Safety and Terrorism

Associated Press. "Florida Synagogue Vandalized on Eve of Rosh Hashanah." *OrlandoSentinel.com*. Orlando Sentinel, 03 Oct. 2016. Web. 14 Mar. 2017.

"Baltimore, MD Crime Data and Crime Rates." *NeighborhoodScout.com*. Location Inc. Web. 04 Mar. 2017.

Burke, Daniel. "Bomb Threats Target Dozens of Jewish Centers. Trump Finally Responds." *CNN*. Cable News Network, 27 Feb. 2017. Web. 14 Mar. 2017.

Dave, Aussie. ""How A Trip to Israel Changed My Perception of Israelis"." *Israellycool.com*. Israellycool, 25 Aug. 2016. Web. 04 Mar. 2017.

Diamond, Jeremy. "Donald Trump Disavows 'alt-right'." *CNN*. Cable News Network, 23 Nov. 2016. Web. 04 Mar. 2017.

Dzik, Steven. "The United Nations Has Broken All Its Promises to Israel." *Algemeiner.com*. The Algemeiner, 8 Jan. 2017. Web. 04 Mar. 2017.

Edelhart, Sophie, Eliza Moss-Horwitz, and Jack Snyder. "Unlearning Apartheid Apologism: A Jewish Response to Israeli Apartheid Week." *Columbia Daily Spectator*. Spectator Publishing Company, 5 Mar. 2017. Web. 20 Mar. 2017.

"European Antisemitism from Its Origins to the Holocaust." *Ushmm.org*. United States Holocaust Memorial Museum. Web. 04 Mar. 2017.

Frank, Anne. *Anne Frank: The Diary of a Young Girl*. Glenview, IL: Scott Foresman Addison Wesley, 2001. Print.

Friedman, Matti. "What the Media Gets Wrong About Israel." *The Atlantic*. Atlantic Media Company, 30 Nov. 2014. Web. 04 Mar. 2017.

Frommer, Rachel. "San Diego Student Says Her View of Israel as 'Akin to Apartheid' Completely Changed After Visiting Jewish State." *Algemeiner.com*. The Algemeiner, 20 Jan. 2017. Web. 13 Mar. 2017.

Gurion, David Ben, Yehuda Leib Fishman, Aharon Zisling, and Moshe Shertok. "Proclamation of Independence." *Knesset.gov.il*. The State of Israel, 2003. Web. 21 Apr. 2017.

Hughbanks, Vivian. "UN Claims Jews Have No Significant Ties To Jerusalem." *Thefederalist.com*. The Federalist, 25 Oct. 2016. Web. 04 Mar. 2017.

Islamic Resistance Movement. "The Charter of the Hamas." *Acpr.org*. Ariel Center for Policy Research. Web. 21 Apr. 2017.

Kalman, Matthew. "Palestinian Teaches Tolerance via Holocaust." *The New York Times*. The New York Times, 20 Apr. 2014. Web. 13 Mar. 2017.

Liebermann, Oren. "Jews Leave France in Record Numbers." *CNN*. Cable News Network, 25 Jan. 2016. Web. 04 Mar. 2017.

Lillywhite, James. "A Gaza Store Named 'Hitler 2' Has Just Put Knife-wielding Mannequins on Display." *International Business Times UK*. IBTimesco. 05 Nov. 2015. Web. 13 Mar. 2017.

Lozada, Carlos. "Opinion | Donald Trump and the Alt-right: A Marriage of Convenience." *The Washington Post*. WP Company, 30 Dec. 2016. Web. 04 Mar. 2017.

Rector, Kevin. "Deadliest Year in Baltimore History Ends with 344 Homicides." *Baltimoresun.com*. Baltimore Sun, 09 Aug. 2016. Web. 04 Mar. 2017.

Rosenbaum, Sophia. "New Yorkers Band Together to Clean Swastika-covered Subway Car." *New York Post*. New York Post, 05 Feb. 2017. Web. 14 Mar. 2017.

Snyder, Ron. "Bomb Threats Reported at Owings Mills JCC, Maryland Jewish Day School." *WBAL*. WBAL, 28 Feb. 2017. Web. 13 Mar. 2017.

Steve. "Israel: A Melting Pot of Cultures." *IsraelSeen.com*. IsraelSeen.com, 29 May 2012. Web. 04 Apr. 2017.

"The Aftermath of the Holocaust." *Ushmm.org*. United States Holocaust Memorial Museum. Web. 04 Mar. 2017.

"Theodor (Binyamin Zeev) Herzl." *Jewish Virtual Library.* Jewish Virtual Library. Web. 19 Mar. 2017.

"U.N. Votes for Partition of Palestine." *History.com.* A&E Television Networks. Web. 19 Mar. 2017.

Where I'm From

"Jack Greenberg." *Naacpldf.org.* NAACP Legal Defense and Education Fund Inc. Web. 04 Mar. 2017.

Some Jewish History

"About Us." *Jewishagency.org.* The Jewish Agency. Web. 04 Mar. 2017.

"A Timeline of the History of Israel." *Contenderministries.org.* Web. 04 Mar. 2017.

Bitton, Jimmy. "History of the Yellow Jewish Star." *Jewishmag.com.* Jewish Magazine. Web. 04 Mar. 2017.

"Historical Timeline: 1900-Present - Israeli-Palestinian Conflict - ProCon.org." *Procon.org.* Procon.org, 22 July 2015. Web. 04 Mar. 2017.

Nix, Elizabeth. "What Was the Dreyfus Affair?" *History.com.* A&E Television Networks, 14 Jan. 2015. Web. 04 Mar. 2017.

"Timeline." *Astro.temple.edu.* Temple University. Web. 04 Mar. 2017.

"U.N. Security Council: The Meaning of Resolution 242." *Jewish Virtual Library.* American-Israeli Cooperative Enterprise. Web. 11 Mar. 2017.

"19th Century Anti-Semitism." *Alphahistory.com.* Alpha History, 18 May 2016. Web. 04. Mar. 2017.

About the Author

Elana Rubin was born in Livingston, New Jersey, and currently lives in Pikesville, Maryland with her parents and twin siblings, across the street from her grandparents. She attended Jewish Day School from preschool to eighth grade, with the exception of sixth grade, when she lived in Ramat Aviv Gimel, Israel. For high school, she attended the Literary Arts program at George Washington Carver Center for the Arts and Technology. She was an editor for the *Synergy* literary magazine, where her poetry is published in three editions. Her work was also included in the World Artists Experiences anthology in 2015. She has had success with the Jack London Foundation Writing Competition and the Scholastics Arts and Writing Regional Competition, where she won five gold keys, including in writing portfolio. In the fall, she will attend Johns Hopkins University, where she will major in Writing Seminars. This is her first book, and she plans to write many more.

Made in the USA
Columbia, SC
28 October 2017